Sanctuary

Other Books by Terry Hershey

The Power of Pause: Becoming More by Doing Less

Soul Gardening

Sanctuary

creating a space for
grace in your life

TERRY HERSHEY

LOYOLA PRESS.
A JESUIT MINISTRY
Chicago

LOYOLA PRESS.
A JESUIT MINISTRY

3441 N. Ashland Avenue
Chicago, Illinois 60657
(800) 621-1008
www.loyolapress.com

Cover art credit: ©iStock/Rach27

Back cover author photo, Judith A. Hinderer.

Hardcover

ISBN-13: 978-0-8294-4264-9
ISBN-10: 0-8294-4264-2

Paperback

ISBN-13: 978-0-8294-4357-8
ISBN-10: 0-8294-4357-6
Library of Congress Control Number: 2014959303

Printed in the United States of America.

15 16 17 18 19 20 RRD 10 9 8 7 6 5 4 3 2 1

To my grandmother Gladys Thelma Andrews

Contents

It Began
with a Porch
Swing

IN THE LATTER YEARS OF HER LIFE, in the backyard of her home in northern Florida, my grandmother had a porch swing. She liked to sit and swing and hum old church hymns such as "Rock of Ages, Cleft for Me." I can still see her there, wearing a white scarf over her head, a concession to chemotherapy's unrelenting march. When as a young adult I visited her, she would always ask me to sit with her on the swing for a spell. She would pat my leg and call me "darlin'."

As long as my grandmother lived—and in spite of her pain—there was always a place for me on the swing. If I were asked to explain grace, I would paint the picture of my grandmother's swing. There, I never had to deliberate or explain or worry, regardless of the weight I carried. The porch swing—my grandmother's presence—bestowed grace without conditions.

And I am here today because of that porch swing. I am here today because of a sanctuary.

Everyone has a sanctuary, if only in the mind. Even if we can't say what it is, we know of its power. It is a place where we feel grounded, unhurried, and renewed. We go there whenever we can, which never seems often enough. Or that's what we tell ourselves.

A sanctuary is a place that restores us, replenishes us, nourishes us. In this renewal, we are reminded, once again, of what really is important.

We are wired to need grounding and renewal. Yes, I believe it's in our emotional DNA. So you'd think creating sanctuary would be at the top of our priorities. But there's the sticky wicket. We end up making choices—with our time and with our days—that are detrimental to our emotional and spiritual well-being.

If I had my druthers, I'd put my pen down (yes, I still write with a fountain pen) and invite you to take a walk with me. We're not going far. Off to the side of my garden and tucked under a maple tree is a swing. It's for cogitating and sitting for a spell.

I can tell the weeks when I do not get my recommended dose of sanctuary—or in my case, garden time. And I can tell when I do take my sanctuary time because it restores me; it's a dose of grace mainlined straight to the heart.

In her book *The Sabbath World*, Judith Shulevitz quotes a lovely teaching by the eighteenth-century master the Vilna Gaon. "Consider the mystery surrounding the first Shabbat. Why did God stop, anyway? God stopped to show us that what we create becomes meaningful only once we stop creating it and start remembering why it was worth creating in the first place." Shulevitz closes by saying, "We have to remember to stop because we have to stop to remember."

We stop to create sanctuary. In sanctuary, we let life in—every bit of life, wholeheartedly, whether that is grief or sadness or bewilderment or gladness or joy.

We make space in which to see and to be seen. We make space to welcome. We make space to be Sabbath in a world of disquiet, disruption, and misgiving. We make space to offer comfort or reprieve or hope.

But how? How do we make that space? Where and when? If you picked up this little book, you probably feel the need for sanctuary. Maybe you have already stumbled upon it. Then again, maybe you need it but can't find it or don't know how to create it. In the chapters to come, we will explore sanctuary together. My hope is that by the end of this journey you will have found and reclaimed sanctuary where it already exists. Also, you will have purposeful ideas about how to create sanctuary right where you live, now.

But I have to warn you. Our journey together of creating sanctuary places will require a shift in the way you think about the concept of sanctuary. It will mean a new way of seeing. Because sanctuary is not a program to add to our to-do list. Sanctuary is a way of life. We may not be good at it or do it "right," or we may give ourselves grief for lacking the willpower to commit and carry through. But who convinced us in the first place that those elements are essential? Is it possible to experience sanctuary when we aren't very successful or correct or strong willed?

For now it is enough to accept this invitation to begin a journey—a journey to create and embrace your sanctuary places, and to visit them often. You will be glad you did.

1

Who Needs Sanctuary, and Why?

I'M EAVESDROPPING, sitting in an airport shuttle, listening to two coworkers unpack their business trip. "It was *sooo* great. I was always on the go. Didn't even get a chance to talk to my husband or kids. So I say to him, I'm *like* . . . sorry."

Ask anyone, "How are you?" The responses range from "super busy" to "crazy busy" to "insanely busy" to "you wouldn't believe it if I told you." Apparently nobody is "just fine" anymore.

My favorite answer, from asking a friend, is this: "I'm overscheduled, overcommitted, and overextended. Does that answer your question?"

"Yes," I tell him. "But the good news is that your alliteration skills have not been affected."

Listening to the women on the shuttle, I smile, knowing that it could be me. Although I'm sure that if *I* am overtaxed, there's a good reason for it. I must deserve it somehow. And yet, I know that, deep down, I don't want to live this way. I know that I need a sanctuary.

Apparently I'm not the only one who needs sanctuary. There are anecdotes aplenty, and studies abound about the general state of things. Details in valuable books such as Carl Honore's *In Praise of Slowness* and Brigid Schulte's *Overwhelmed: Work, Love, and Play When No One Has the Time* reinforce what we all suspect: we are overwhelmed and overextended.

One study cited in the Schulte book, involving eleven experiments and seven hundred people, discovered that a majority of people found it unpleasant to be alone in a room with their thoughts for just six to fifteen minutes. Here's where it gets curious: many people actually preferred physical pain—delivered via tiny doses of electrical shock—to the emotional pain of sitting alone with no distractions.

Crazy? I don't know. You tell me. Are we perpetually on the run from boredom, requiring stimulus for its own sake? Or, when confronted with our busyness, do we assume we can replace it with different activities and exchange one distraction for another?

It's one thing to be bored; it's another to add to the day's obligations the need to feel important or the need to impress or the need to avoid the loneliness that emptiness can bring.

It seems clear that we have trained ourselves to *avoid* sanctuary—that time and place for stillness. But no matter who we are, we need that stillness more than ever. Every last one of us needs the restoration that sanctuary offers. Consider these people; you probably know them, and you're possibly one of them:

- A man or woman in a significant, high-stress job who talks about the toll of the treadmill but is unable to get off
- A mother or father in a family that's doing all right but whose long days and many responsibilities bring on anxiety, fatigue, and the recurring sense that something is missing

- A recently divorced man or woman who feels betrayed and abandoned and whose anger is getting the better of him or her
- A single parent living in a small apartment with high-spirited kids and no disposable income
- A person employed by the church who is overworked, underpaid, undervalued, with fewer resources every year, and who feels unsupported and exhausted
- Someone of modest means who lives in a rural small town, where nothing happens, and who sees the same people day in and day out
- A wealthy couple who began life together dreaming of changing the world for the better but have fallen into the pattern of simply seeking "peak moments" in travel, which are wonderful but are starting to feel empty
- An elderly couple who live on a fixed income, whose local church community has dwindled over the years to just a few dozen people, who have seen important friends and family die one by one, and who fear that the world they've known and belonged to is fading before their eyes
- A thirty-something who suspects there might be more to life but who finds him- or herself constantly attached to a smartphone, a tablet, television, video games, or social media

- A person or couple at the end of the career years, or at the beginning of the empty-nest years—a time of transition when there is anxiety about what is next and sometimes a feeling of marginalization
- A person who has given the past five years of his or her life caring for aging or declining parents, all while juggling job, marriage, and caregiver roles, feeling the constant pressure of responsibility but also feeling unappreciated
- A newly married couple, their heads full of dreams and goals, facing an unexpected turn of fortune or loss of income
- A couple who are doing just fine—with the right jobs, a home, hobbies, and relationships—but who carry a sense of discomfort and the nagging question, "When is enough, enough?"
- A person who enjoys work, family, and finds life fulfilling but who still needs a time and place to be still

What does your own story look like? You can add it to this list. What do you imagine having sanctuary could add to this already-full life of yours?

We are on this journey to name and embrace sanctuaries—places of grace. Along this journey, some of us have named our sanctuaries. Some of us have discovered a place that has been there all along.

Hurry, Hurry

We're on the go, shuttling kids to soccer or music lessons, or taking ourselves to meetings (it's Tuesday, so it must be church) or errands. And when there *is* time for reflection, out comes the mobile device. It's a permanent reflex now, isn't it? I've sometimes wondered if we've become a nation of prayer; because in any public space, everyone has his or her head bowed, scrutinizing a phone or other electronic screen.

I once heard someone confess, "I would *love* to have one uninterrupted hour." I heard this while sitting in an airport departure lounge. Our plane had been delayed, and we had—wait for it—*one hour* to kill.

Daily, we are marinated in speed—so much so that our minds have been rewired. So much so that we believe instant gratification takes too long. We live in a world where fast-food restaurants have express lines; our bookstores carry the title *One-Minute Bedtime Stories*; and if you need to relax but are pinched for time, there's a speed yoga class. And don't get me started on the church that has "drive-through" communion. No, I'm not making that up.

This much is true: undivided is precisely what attention is *not*. Speed and hurry take their toll. Our headlong dash does damage to the soul. Sometimes we just need to vent. And sometimes we genuinely want relief or guidance. Sadly, it is usually a wake-up call—illness, misfortune—that puts us on the road to change.

It's Not Just about Speed

It is too easy to make our need for sanctuary only about speed. Yes, we move too fast. Yes, our lives are hectic and chockablock. But this busyness is about not only more stuff and crammed calendars; it is also about our spiritual and emotional space—where we come face-to-face with the "addictive element" of being too full. I readily grumble about exhaustion. And yet . . .

- my world of obligations fills with my need to fix or impress others.
- my spirit—unnerved by life's uncertainties—becomes a magnet for (and is weighed down by) fear or worry.
- my sense of self and identity attach to pain or loss or unrealized expectations.

What does this mean? This pattern takes care of something: I am filling up my time and interior space out of a need that is real and relentless.

But when my senses are numbed by noise and overload and worry, I am impoverished. I become a man (in the words of Leonardo da Vinci) who "looks without seeing, listens without hearing, touches without feeling, eats without tasting, moves without physical awareness, inhales without awareness of odour or fragrance, and talks without thinking." Filling space becomes the new normal. I am overflowing, overwhelmed, overextended.

Creating sanctuary involves not only welcoming stillness but also making space. And usually, the way we make space is by letting go of something.

In her book *Broken Open*, Elizabeth Lesser talks about our need to "practice death"; this is a process of letting go of whatever enslaves us. I can do this during those moments when I need to take a breath or two, to clear my mind of emotional storm clouds. In that space and moment,

- I no longer need to clutch.
- I no longer need to be a warrior doing battle, as if my identity were dependent only on being strong.
- I choose to quit trying to be perfect or always right or impressive or unflawed or in a hurry.
- If something is toxic to my spirit, I choose to say, "Let it die."
- What I am is enough. I can simply be.

This is the power of making space. Within that space, we are able to see and to receive, even if that means receiving sadness or loss or grief or the death of expectations. You know: *By now I expected to be* _____ (fill in the blank).

Where We Are Truly Home

It's already long past departure time. I'm standing near the gate, waiting for the inbound passengers to deplane. There's nowhere to go, and the plane will depart when it departs. Even so, the passengers (including me) are beginning to huddle, as if our hovering will speed up the process. We form a makeshift column, all of us wanting dibs on the precious overhead-bin cargo space.

Standing nearby, facing the now-open Jetway door, is a uniformed soldier. He stands with nervous energy, conveying a restless and eager air. He watches the door intently. He holds a large poster-board sign, stenciled by hand in permanent marker: "Welcome Home! I love you!"

Since he has been allowed to stand at the arrival gate (past airport security), it is evident that he is waiting for an unaccompanied minor. The passengers from the inbound flight spill from the doorway. She is the final passenger to deplane, accompanied by a flight attendant. Around her neck hangs a plastic packet, which holds her documents. She is preteen, with two perfect braids. She scans the faces, sees her father, and breaks into a radiant and luminous smile.

There is a moment, a pause. And she catapults herself into his wide-open arms. His hand-lettered sign has dropped from his hand to the floor, now immaterial, and as his daughter leans into his chest, he clutches her tightly and kisses her head. Those of us lucky enough to witness this scene know the healing power and blessedness of this embrace.

No. We do not know their entire story. How long since their last visit? Why have they been separated? Has he been deployed and in harm's way? Does she live in another state, unable to visit her father frequently?

But this we do know: every single one of us in that departure lounge wished to be in that embrace. In that embrace, the little girl was at home.

Your Sanctuary

What to you feels like that gigantic hug and welcome? When do you know that you've come home? Finish this sentence for yourself: "I know I've come home when . . ."
   Now, consider these questions.

- How would you describe your life and your world—your relationships, your family, your hobbies, your stresses, your passions?
- When and where do you feel overwhelmed?
- When do you know that you need time and space to replenish? What keeps you from making time for that space?
- If you could make the time and space to replenish, what would that look like?

Now, finish these sentences:

- "I need sanctuary because . . ."
- "Sometimes I choose to live overwhelmed because . . ."
- "If I could freely choose, my sanctuary would include (or incorporate or involve or embody) . . ."

_____

_____

_____

_____

_____

_____

_____

_____

_____

_____

_____

_____

_____

_____

_____

_____

_____

_____

_____

_____

_____

2

What
Sanctuary Is
and What It's Not

JOHN AND JOANIE HAVE BEEN MARRIED FOR FIFTY YEARS. Now they are retired from work, and happily so. John was a rector and Joanie an organist and music director. They are both familiar with the irony that working in a place that is ministry or service oriented can be the antithesis of sanctuary.

"Where is your sanctuary?" I ask. We're on their patio looking out at their garden.

"You're in it," they tell me. "When we found this house and land, we knew. This place is a gift. It felt life giving. We enjoy going places, but we always feel bad about leaving our home. Our soul resides here."

"What makes it unique?" I ask.

"It's not just a house. Here we find our solace—that may sound odd—because we love to tend our garden. We feel like stewards of a special place. It's life giving. When we started building the garden [pathways through trees, a little statue of St. Francis, and a small fountain], we had no idea what the outcome would be; but we were open to the process and heart space. A surprise: we discovered a quiet that, literally, we could sink into."

Sanctuary is a dose of grace. Sanctuary space bestows upon us gifts—stillness, gladness, calm, mystery, delight, and peacefulness. It's not easy for most of us to take grace as our starting point. When it comes to personal or spiritual growth, we often spend our energy chasing or anticipating. But sanctuary begins when we stop and embrace what is already here, when we receive what has already been bestowed on us.

Here's the good news: we can't orchestrate or procure these gifts that come from sanctuary—or magically make them appear through heroic willpower. What we can do is create sanctuary, a space in which the gifts can materialize.

If achieving renewal through sanctuary is the only assumed objective, then I should be giving you a hard sales pitch about now—to toe the line, do it right. And off we go, in pursuit of a newer and more polished self. "If you want less stress, try meditation, yoga, prayer, silent retreat . . ."

But it's not a more polished self we're after when we go to sanctuary.

I started my week on Vashon Island, Washington State, where I live, and today I am in Washington, DC. I spent part of the day with a friend touring the Catoctin Creek Distilling Company in Purcellville, Virginia. It is a perfect sanctuary tour; we learn the value of pausing to let "spirits" age.

As I write this, I look out on the monument that memorializes the lives lost in the attack on the Pentagon. I think about gratitude dancing through open windows. In the middle of the week in Oklahoma, I spent one morning driving the back roads early, the rising sun a molten globe resting on the edge of the world. Morning mist still rose from the fields, which were dotted with plump spools of hay. To the south a murmuration of birds, thousands of them playing, diving, and dancing.

From the speakers of my car, Patti Griffin sang, "You can go wherever you want to go."

Sometimes we go and go, and the constant motion works against us. So we create sanctuary in the car or even the hotel room. Travel is part of my work; usually it's an airplane. For you it may be a car—you alone on the freeway that's become a parking lot, or you in a minivan filled with kids. There are days or weeks when we may not find ourselves in the environment we wish for or choose or need—I have to travel, but a plane seat is not my ideal place to create sanctuary. While I may not be able to control the environment, as I can in my home or garden, I can still be intentional about my mind-set.

Making a place for sanctuary is not easy for me, and certainly it doesn't happen all the time. But I can tell you this: When I pause and am a recipient of moments—even driving the back roads of Oklahoma—there is gladness. In my mind, I'm giving thanks. On my face, there's usually a grin. In my heart, I'm seeing the sacred in the very ordinary.

These are practices I have in my sanctuary—in my garden. And I do practice them when I am there. But here's the good news: I can use these practices, even if only for a moment, wherever I may be. My practice is to pretend my eyes are a camera. I look. I take a deep breath. And then I blink, as if my eyes were camera shutters and I'm taking a picture.

What are some of the gifts of sanctuary?

- Sanctuary allows me to slow down, to stop.

- Sanctuary makes space—exterior and interior—for my soul to catch up with my body.
- Sanctuary gives me permission to say no to the need to achieve or to "be on" or to check an item off a list.
- Sanctuary helps me let go of the need for my identity to be tied to performance or productivity.
- Sanctuary gives me permission to tend to things that really matter.
- Sanctuary allows me the permission for soul care and replenishment.
- Sanctuary is a place where I don't owe anyone and no one owes me.
- Sanctuary is a place where I feel at home in my own skin.
- Sanctuary is a place where I know I am grounded. It connects me to *this* place and *this* time.

In sanctuary . . .

- I tell myself the truth.
- I don't need to pretend to be someone else.
- I am not afraid of imperfection.
- I am not afraid of joy.
- The windows to all my emotions open.
- I feel connected to (or am a part of) something bigger.
- I have nothing to prove.

- A weight is lifted from my shoulders.
- My value is not up for grabs.
- I have space for self-awareness.

In some ways, creating sanctuary is a form of civil disobedience. Slowing down, stopping, making space, saying no, letting go—all of this goes against the grain of the culture in which we've been shaped.

It is true that restoration, rejuvenation, and replenishment can happen without sanctuary. Leisure and vacation have a purpose. (Although we do not sufficiently appreciate leisure and vacation either. It's probably not a surprise to you that we take less vacation than our parents did.)

My grandmother's swing—while restorative—was not a vacation. It recalibrated my soul. And where there is sustenance for the soul, there is sanctuary.

It's important to remember, though, what sanctuary is not.

Sanctuary is not always easy or fun.

In an episode of *The West Wing*, C. J. Craig (White House chief of staff) is wired, tense, and distracted. Her love interest shows up, in the middle of the workday, at her White House office, "to take her for a walk." She consents (but not without a fight—you know, so much "to do"). On the walk, she fidgets and asks, "So, what was so important about taking this walk?"

He says, "Just to see."

"Well," she tells him, "this is not the day for it."

I can relate to C. J. I want to live this moment mindful of the sacred, but this is not the day for it—as if there were a special day for it. Sanctuary, like anything else that's truly important, involves making certain choices:

- To be open
- To be available
- To be curious
- To be alive
- To be willing to be surprised by joy

And whenever there's a choice to be made, one of the alternatives is lesser than the other. Do I take this walk and take some deep breaths and receive some moments of joy? Or do I stay at my desk and worry over my fourth list today? Do I spend ten minutes sitting in my "sanctuary" chair and singing my favorite song, or do I spend those minutes shopping online for things I don't even need?

Sometimes the easy thing—the obsessing that comes naturally, or the next mouse click—is not what the soul needs. Sometimes it's more fun to check social media one more time, but our soul longs not for more fun (distraction) but for more peace (settledness).

Sanctuary is not self-improvement.

Sanctuary does not make me a better person or even a better Christian. Its purpose is not to solve problems or to find answers. In fact, when it comes to sanctuary, it's best not to aim at "accomplishing" anything at all.

I'm in downtown Atlanta at a conference for Spiritual Directors International, doing a presentation about how spiritual care is grounded in self-care. I have a window of time and need a haircut. So I take the recommendation of the concierge and find myself in a salon near the hotel. A few minutes later, I am following a young hairdresser toward a chair in the back of the salon.

"Hi, I'm Sharon. You ready?" Her accent is Southern.

"Can you make me look young, distinguished, and handsome?" I ask.

She cocks her head, glances back, and says, "Well . . . I can do young."

One of my philosophies is this: While getting a haircut—an inevitability on par with traveling in airplanes and waiting in line at the bank—conversation is a bother. Just cut my hair and let me go. After all, I have important stuff to do.

But because she made me laugh, I break my rule about staying mute, saying that maybe a buzz cut is in order. I tell Sharon about my father's decision after cancer to enjoy his new hair-free, carefree look.

"I'm a cancer survivor too," she says. "Just finished my chemo."

I wasn't ready for that. Because in my philosophy, if there *is* conversation, these chairs are for small talk only—no different from coffee hour after church.

"I'm sorry," I say. "When did you learn about the cancer, and what kind of treatment did you go through?"

"I had the whole nine yards." She laughs. "Surgery. And then more surgery and then chemo."

We are quiet, except for the sound of scissors.

"It's the best thing that ever happened to me," she adds.

I've heard people say that—about tragedy or loss or heart-break or misfortune—but I am honestly unsure what to think. How can such a statement be true? I do know that something inside us wants (needs) to find a silver lining, a way to make sense of what appears to be an utterly senseless invasion of our body, or life, or world.

I watch her in the mirror. Sharon is young, in her mid-thirties, petite, her facial features delicate and freck-led—she carries a youthful innocence. There is no sign of any recent clash with the chemo drug treatments, which trauma-tize body and spirit all in the name of health.

She looks into the mirror and holds my gaze. "It has made me softer," she tells me. "And now, I love different."

A single mother, Sharon talks about her fifteen-year-old daughter, in a tenor both wistful and filled with pride. She describes a young girl whose life was turned upside down with the possibility of a mother's death, and a renewed relationship between mother and daughter.

I nod. I understand.

"We never know," she continues. "A year ago if you had told me that this is where I'd be, I'd have told you you're crazy. But not now. Now I look at people differently."

I compliment her hair. Quickly realizing my error, I try to apologize.

But Sharon shakes her head, tossing her hair, looking cute and sassy. "Thanks. I made it. It's something I do now. It's my calling. To make personal wigs for people going through chemo so they can look beautiful on the outside and feel beautiful on the inside."

Go figure. I'm at a conference with spiritual directors from different faith traditions around the world, and my moment of enlightenment and grace is gifted to me in a beauty-salon chair.

As a boy, I was taught in church that we should love one another. You know, practice kindness and compassion. But love can spill only from a heart that has been softened and, in most cases, broken.

In any encounter, including sanctuary moments, if I do give or offer my heart, it comes back to me in better shape. It comes back to me softer. There is no doubt that when we face tragedy or chaos or uncertainty or misfortune, we want to have a "handle" on it, or fix it, or make it go away. But the point is not to get a handle on things, to figure out what has happened and why. Nor is it to determine whether we have intentionally or unintentionally invited chaos or sickness into our world.

The point is to give ourselves permission to see the world—this day—through the eyes of our heart, our heart made soft.

We give ourselves this permission when . . .

- we allow ourselves to feel, fully and wholly, without a need to defend, justify, or explain.
- we allow ourselves to receive love and kindness without suspicion.
- we are free to embrace the core of strength and courage that resides inside of us and then let it spill over to those around us.

After the conference someone asked me, "What did you do there?"

Well, I got a haircut. And I felt my heart soften just a little.

Sanctuary is not for spiritual overachievers.

Dewitt Jones tells a story about visiting Marion Campbell, considered the finest weaver in all of Scotland. She lived in the Outer Hebrides. Jones visited there to photograph Marion for *National Geographic*. When she answered the door, she seemed surprised—no wonder, considering that the Hebrides are a remote island chain, the whole string of sixty-five islands with fewer than twenty-seven thousand inhabitants. I expect she didn't see a stranger very often. Marion told Dewitt, "I'm sorry, but now I am taking care of my brother who is sick and near death." Dewitt felt an understandable embarrassment.

"No, wait," she told him. "Give me an hour. I'll join you then."

After the hour, he found her at the loom. She talked about her creations and told stories about scraping lichen from rocks for dye. Dewitt took a few photos. Still nervous that he had interrupted Marion, he started to leave. "Oh, no," she told him. She escorted him into her dining room, where she had put out biscuits and tea. Dewitt wondered if he was in the presence of a great sage, and he waited to hear pearls of wisdom. "What do you think about when you weave?" he asked.

"I wonder if I'll run out of thread," she answered. She must have seen the puzzlement on his face, adding, "When I weave, I weave."

There it is. When I read, I read. When I celebrate, I celebrate. When I pay attention, I pay attention.

Sanctuary is not a doctoral program. If you're looking for something like that, you will be disappointed. Sanctuary is not a place where we ponder questions such as, "What if this life of mine is the wrong life?" It's a place not of judgment but of acceptance. Have I done boneheaded things in my life? To be sure. Have I miscalculated and misused talent or opportunity? Assuredly. Does it benefit me to wish that I were elsewhere and otherwise? I don't think so. Sanctuary allows me to dwell in this life *as it is*.

There is something about our need to see a payoff for our efforts, isn't there? As if we can overcome this awkward part of our life. But awkward or inconvenient or downright intolerable, we are offered an invitation. What Martin Heidegger called *Dasein*, or "being in the world"—a reference not to existence but to our capacity to enter fully into the day, this day.

Sanctuary is not only for the times when we've reached the end of our rope.

It is quite true that there can be a cathartic release in just shutting down, telling whoever is close by or shouting to the heavens, "I've had enough. I'm closed *now!*" There is nothing wrong with that.

Sometimes we do need the ER—whether for our bodies or for our spirits. We need to find someone who knows CPR, just to get the heart pumping again. Although there is some kind of stubborn satisfaction from the adrenaline rush we get from pushing ourselves too far, deep down we know different, and we need an opportunity to be gentle with ourselves before it's too late.

We all know by now that good preventative care is a much better strategy than poor health care, which will land us, one fateful day, in the ER. Sanctuary is good when we've reached the end of our rope and our resources. But it's even better as part of ongoing life practices.

Tonight was the final performance of *Through the Garden Gate* at Vashon's Blue Heron Art Center—the piece features a remarkable collaborative of local talent walking through the seasons of a garden. In my role I say:

> People who love this world, people who pay attention, are gardeners, whether or not they have ever picked up a trowel. Because gardening is not just about digging. Or planting for that matter. Gardening is about cherishing. And to cherish, we must be present.
>
> Here in the Pacific Northwest, the wet and the gray and the dark get old. But if we are honest, winter does us a favor. It's been said that when the supports are gone, we can find where our real worth lies. Not exactly what we have in mind, but so it is. An invitation to stop, to listen, to take a deep breath, to hunker down and chew the cud with no need to come up with any answers because none are required. It is an invitation seldom taken, because to stop may mean facing some discomfort about choices we've made, relationships and friends that we've lost, or the reality that we're not nearly where we thought we should be. But the truth is that after all our moaning and moping, we come one day to enjoy our own company, and embrace the reality that we are, after all, human. And that is not such a bad place to be. So we curl up on the couch with a cup of tea and a good book, or a daydream if we have one. On one such afternoon, we happen to glance to see the very first light of spring, still low in the sky, but buoyant and hope filled, shafts of light slanting through the cathedral spires of hemlock, cedar, and fir.

That kind of attentiveness, of presence, can be our daily, year-long sanctuary, if we let it.

Sanctuary is not complete removal from life.

It's not as if I go from life to sanctuary and then back again. When on retreat, we often say to ourselves, "I wish my real life could be like this!" And as we reenter "real life," we say that we are going "back to the grind."

I remember perusing the shelves of one of my favorite independent bookstores some time back and finding a title that gave me pause: *U-Turn: What If You Woke Up One Morning and Realized You Were Living the Wrong Life?* (Mercy—this is a good way to throw a monkey wrench into any fine weekend. I mean, should I cancel dinner reservations?)

I sensed that the author could be right, that this applied to my own life, which led to an uncomfortable scene in the bookstore, with me on the floor, being consoled by a minimum-wage store clerk, who may or may not be living the right life, which seemed beyond my capacity to discern—she was very helpful nonetheless, patting me on the head and saying, "There, there," and giving me the name of a nearby pub that specialized in soothing middle-aged angst.

What if I'm living the wrong life? It is a question we all entertain, and it gnawed at me over that weekend. This seems to be a riddle for someone with way too much time on his or her hands. Which brings me to today, which started as I begin most every day when I'm at home:

- I made a pot of coffee.
- I journaled for a half hour.
- I walked the garden as my morning invocation, periodically checking for raccoon damage.
- I intended to write about what the "right life" looks like but was preoccupied for a good deal of time by the way the morning dew weighted the new late-summer blossoms on the Penelope rose. From the recent rain, the lawn is Irish green and the black-eyed Susans lean (or bow? in deference or in reverence?) from the heaviness of the rain.

I was, truly, mesmerized. And gratefully, I reentered my life.

Sanctuary does not take us out of the life we have; it makes a way for us to love and savor the life we have.

Yes. Are we ready? Let's begin the journey.

3

Where Do We
Find
Sanctuary?

Susan's schedule makes me dizzy, or envious, of all the energy she has. Mother of three—ages eight to thirteen—she is taxi driver, calendar coordinator, cook, consoler, house supervisor, and bottle washer. Susan's husband commutes to work, leaving the house early and returning late, carried by the tide of freeway traffic. Susan also volunteers—at the local school and at her church, and she is involved in a local garden club.

I ask her about sanctuary. She gives me a wistful look and says, "I wish." And then she adds, "I'll have time someday. That's the good news. I just need to get through these years."

I believe her, and I know what it means to wait for better times before making plans for sanctuary. I ask her what she does when she has a small window of "Susan time." Her answer is immediate: "A cappuccino in the breakfast nook off our kitchen that looks out at the bird feeders. I start making lists. But some days I just stare off or doodle. I love to doodle and sketch the birds I see. It's nothing really."

We don't give ourselves the permission to claim or own or embrace or name our sanctuaries, no matter how small or frivolous they may seem.

Sanctuary is where you go to cherish your life. It's where you practice being present. And it may not be that many steps from where you are, right now.

So. Where is your sacred place?

No worries if you can't name it. We'll get there. In the meantime, it helps to remember that we do not go there . . .

- Merely to fulfill an obligation
- Just to be a good person
- To impress people we know

We go there because if we don't go, we lose a part of our soul.

I used to think I had to go somewhere special—exotic maybe. Or maybe I just wanted a change of scenery, a wave of a magic wand making all the litter in my life go away. And I confess that I still am mesmerized by bucket-list books and the ten thousand places I need to go before I die.

I guess I assumed that I could enjoy sanctuary only with the change of scenery, as if sanctuary couldn't happen in my real world.

I remember a wonderful conversation with Luanne, a patient in hospice at a local senior center. At age ninety-three, she still carried herself with dignity and poise, even if the facts of the day were sometimes muddled and jumbled. "It's my teatime," she tells me. "Excuse me?" I ask. "Oh," she says, "I have a special tea. I can sit up for about thirty minutes, so I have the nurse help me to the chair by the window, where I sip my tea." She is smiling, and I know that even in this room surrounded by medical equipment, sanctuary can be found.

I think through my own day. Sometimes my mind just goes blank. And I want to choose and find sanctuary, but then

I wonder whether I'm doing it *correctly*. This is for certain: I can tell the days I don't have my teatime.

It can help if we ask ourselves a simple question: *What is saving me today?*

For me, today, it is my garden. I am in my garden. I will write my pressing project later tonight. For now:

- I am not phoning.
- I am not blogging.
- I am not Twittering.
- I am not texting.
- I am not e-mailing.
- I am not mentally editing a to-do list in my head.
- I *am* resting.

Your sanctuary might be a lot different from mine. But there is some place in your life that feels safer, less frenetic, and truer than other places. You might not have a lot of free time—between one or more jobs, kids and other family members to care for, responsibilities in your community. And it's easy to get off track trying to master the game of balancing life. But there are certain times of the day or week in which you're actually alone and it's either too late at night or early in the morning for anyone else to need you. Or that bit of time in the afternoon after one shift of life has ended and before the next one has begun.

Ideally, each and every one of us could find sanctuary in some beautiful place away from hurry and care. In Seattle, with our gray and rain, we are envious of anyone with exotic sunshine. Indeed, there are times when I've found sanctuary in Hawaii. But there are other times when I've gone to Hawaii and found just sunburn. In reality, many of us have to learn how to recognize sanctuary closer to home.

The setting alone doesn't make the sanctuary. It's also what we bring to that space: our true desires, our honest feelings, our willingness to open heart and mind. I do know this—if you don't bring it with you, you won't find it there.

Where do you choose to find sanctuary?

Sixty-four Stanford students escape from the campus hustle and find tranquility in a class for two hours a week in the lower level of a campus library. They might start class by telling the person next to them about a positive experience from the day or by updating their gratitude journals. They might simply close their eyes and sit silently, concentrating on relaxing tense muscles and breathing deeply.

"These students are stressed," course instructor Fred Luskin says. "They're all high achievers, but they don't know how to turn off that drive. The consequences are exhaustion, a sense of feeling older than your peers, and lack of relationships. This class helps them learn that they can be productive without the wear and tear." Students have often described this popular course as their "most valuable class."

One of the best things about sanctuary is that it can happen in the middle of sorrow and hardship. Sometimes we don't understand that until we are forced by circumstance.

Robben Island is famous. It is the South African prison where Nelson Mandela and many others were incarcerated because of their struggle to end apartheid. (Mandela served eighteen of his twenty-seven years in prison in Robben Island.) The writer Margaret Wheatley tells a story of a time she had the unique privilege of touring Robben Island (now a UNESCO World Heritage site).

The tour group stood in a long, narrow room that had been used as a prison cell for dozens of freedom fighters. Picture yourself in a space crowded, cramped, and barren. The prisoners lived without cots or furniture, cement floors for a bed. The only light entered through slender windows near the ceiling.

The tour group listened to the guide's narration. "I was a prisoner in this very room," he tells them. The gravity of his words mingles with the cold seeping up through the floor. There is a chill.

The group stares through prison bars, surveys the lifeless cell, and tries to imagine suffering from relentless threats and capricious brutality.

The guide pauses, as if remembering, gazing the length of his former cell. Speaking quietly, almost a whisper, he says,

"Sometimes, to pass the time here, we taught each other ballroom dancing."

When I first read Wheatley's story, I wasn't ready for that ending. Even with the gut-wrenching bleakness, I confess to grinning, and then laughing out loud.

Ballroom dancing? A group of demoralized and weary men, beaten down and brutalized, teaching one another to dance. You gotta love it.

And yes, we know that it is wiser to light a candle than to curse the darkness. But let's be honest. Sometimes life is dark and not fun. Adversity is real. Life can be cruel. (People can be crueler.) Suffering happens. Suffering hurts. We reach a tipping point. And prison walls are made of real concrete. And finding a candle is not always easy, let alone the motivation to light it.

That's why I love this story—it is so counterintuitive. Let me get this straight: in times of anxiety or fear or suffering or distress—when our equilibrium is catawampus, when we want to go away, or get away from it all—we are invited to open our heart? We are invited to dance? The prisoners would say yes. They would say that in adversity, the medicine of intimacy allows us to become more human; that even times of sorrow or discontent can become fertile ground for generosity of spirit, mystery, delight, touch, tenderness, vulnerability, risk, and—yes—even gladness.

It doesn't make immediate sense to us to make ourselves vulnerable, to open up to what might happen, because our tendency is to shut down. To let our heart constrict. To appear tough and self-sufficient. To find safe haven. To, at the very least, find an enemy—stress, obligations, lists. With an enemy, at least there is someone to blame for all this muddle. The irony is that in every choice between openness and self-protection (and they are choices), we relinquish our very ability to choose.

Our heart tells us to resonate with this yearning to dance. And then we hope that someone will provide us with detailed instructions, a checklist. Because with instructions, *we will learn to dance correctly.*

Somehow, we do not believe that the dance—the perseverance, the light, the tenderness, the intimacy, the wholeheartedness—is already within us.

This is the way it happened to me.

I did not set out to find answers, health, the good life, or even God. In fact, I did not "set out" at all. I know only that my soul felt malnourished. Then one day I found myself in the garden, and quite without fanfare, the journey began.

Life begins to germinate when the ground is fertile and primed.

To repeat a few lines of the community play: "People who love this world, people who pay attention, are gardeners, whether or not they have ever picked up a trowel, because gardening is not just about digging. Or planting for that matter. Gardening is about cherishing. And to cherish, one must be present."

Remember, sanctuary is where you go to cherish your life. It's where you practice being present. And it may not be that many steps from where you are, right now.

Your Sanctuary

Try some journaling time now. Play around with these questions.

- What nourishes you—what do you love?
- What sustains you—gives you balance and equilibrium?
- What inspires you—keeps the fire going or keeps you from being stuck?
- What satisfies you—gives you comfort or small pleasures?
- Where do you give back—where do you find meaning?
- Where have you found sanctuary—even in sorrow?
- What makes you love life—gives you joy and pride?
- What are you grateful for—where does your belief reside?
- Try to recall a time when you discovered sanctuary. What happened? What story would you share?

_____

_____

_____

_____

4
New
Eyes

*Your assumptions are your windows on the world. Scrub them off
every once in a while, or the light won't come in.*

—Alan Alda

I'M ON A PLANE, IN A CONVERSATION WITH MY SEATMATE. Raul
is a government worker and has been in his career for more
than twenty years. He is an engineer, a job that requires dili-
gence, analytical skills, and attentiveness. It's serious work.
His personality matches his profession: steady, cautious, and
reliable.

His is a very predictable world. He tells me that he's married, his children are grown, and he's expecting a grandchild
soon. He's looking forward to that. Even his tone is unhurried
and deliberate.

"So," I ask him, "tell me something about you that people
wouldn't guess."

There's a long pause. "When I was young, I was a compet-
itive roller skater."

I was ready for just about anything, but roller-skating? Not
a chance. We talked about it, and I reminisced about my youth
and the skating parties, and that feeling in the pit of your
stomach as you wonder if the cute girl will choose you to skate
with her during "ladies' choice."

"I don't compete anymore," he says. "But I still skate." I
can tell his mind is there now, as he adds, "When I skate, it's
the only time in my life when I feel graceful. And the only time
I feel truly free."

No, he didn't use the word *sanctuary*. But it is.

According to Omid Safi, director of the Duke University Islamic Studies Center, in many Muslim cultures, your greeting is, "Kayf haal-ik?" in Arabic, or "Haal-e shomaa chetoreh?" in Persian languages. How is your *haal*? But what is this *haal*? It is the transient state of one's heart. In reality, we ask, "How is your heart doing at this very moment, at this breath?" When I ask, "How are you?" that is really what I want to know.

I am not asking how many items are on your to-do list, nor am I asking how many items are in your inbox. I want to know how your heart is doing at this very moment. Tell me. Tell me your heart is joyous, tell me your heart is aching, tell me your heart is sad, tell me your heart craves a human touch. Examine your own heart, explore your soul, and then tell me something about your heart and your soul.

A sanctuary is a place to rejuvenate, renew, retreat, refresh, relax, restore, replenish . . .

- I go to my sanctuary to let the cares of the day dissipate.
- I go to my sanctuary to listen to my heart.
- I go to my sanctuary to regain my soul.
- I go to my sanctuary to hear the voice of grace.

I heard a Tibetan story once about an earnest young man seeking enlightenment. A famous sage passes through the man's village. The man asks the sage to teach him the art of meditation. The sage agrees. He tells the man, "Withdraw from the world. Meditate every day in the specific way I will teach you. Do not waver, and you will attain enlightenment."

The earnest man follows the sage's instructions to the letter. Time passes—and no enlightenment. Two years pass, then five, ten, twenty.

It happens that the sage once again passes through the man's village. The man seeks him out, grumbling that despite his best intentions and devotion and diligent efforts, he has not achieved enlightenment. "Why?"

The sage asks the man, "What meditation did I teach you?"

The man tells him.

The sage says, "Oh, what a terrible mistake I made! That is not the right meditation for you. You should have done another kind altogether. Too bad, for now it is too late."

Disconsolate, the man returns to his cave. Staking his life on the sage's instructions, and believing himself to be without hope, the man abandons all his wishes and efforts and the need to control his road to enlightenment. He does not know what to do. So, he does what he knows best: he begins meditating. And in a short while, much to his astonishment, his confusion begins to dissolve and his inner world comes to life. A weight falls away, and he feels lighter and regenerated. When he walks out of the cave, the sky is bluer, the snowcapped mountains whiter, and the world around him more vivid.

The man seeking enlightenment didn't find it the way he expected; in fact, the harder he tried, the more frustrated he became. It wasn't until his perception shifted that he recognized his enlightenment.

In this chapter, I'll give you a few examples of looking at something with "new eyes"—of experiencing shifts in the way we see and how one small shift can make all the difference.

All too often, our efforts—to succeed or achieve or attain—get in the way of our living. I understand how this happens. I was weaned on a spirituality that placed more importance on appearance than on simply being. It was vital to "look spiritual." Which begs the question, "What do spiritual people look like?" As a boy, I always thought the spiritual people looked as if some part of their clothing was a size too small.

That kind of belief system has a vision problem. What were we holding on to, so rigid and white knuckled in our determination? I know from experience that our perception of spirituality limited us, made us fearful and worried and, eventually, exhausted. At some point, you've got to breathe. Just breathe. And open your eyes, willing to be surprised and awed.

Without realizing it, and after the sage's disheartening news, the man in the story "let go":

- He let go of the need to see life as a problem to be solved.

- He let go of the need to have the correct answers (or experiences) to achieve his "enlightenment."

- He let go of the need to see his spiritual life in terms of a formula.

- He let go of the restraints that come from paying attention to public opinion.

This story brings to mind one of my favorite Leonard Cohen quotes: "Abandon your masterpiece, sink into the real masterpiece."

Without realizing it, the man seeking enlightenment took Leonard Cohen's advice. He abandoned his "masterpiece"—the perception of what he needed to accomplish, or how he needed to appear, or what he needed to feel—and allowed himself to sink down into *this* life, *this* moment, even with all its uncertainty and insecurity.

For the first many years, meditation or prayer was a requirement or compulsion for the man in our story. In his emptiness, meditation and prayer became offerings of thanks, freely given and without constraint. His change is similar to what many of us experience; our transformation seems to happen when we are not trying to impress anyone or score any points with heavenly bookkeepers.

A man dies. An angel is escorting him around. (There is, apparently, the Angelic Hospitality Committee on the other side.) The angel takes him to places where the scenery renders the man speechless.

"I had no idea," the man says.

Emerald-green valleys, rushing rivers cascading over boulders the size of VW buses, sunlight dancing along the landscape, shapes and forms created from the shading in hillside folds, and an endless palette of blues in the sky and in the sea—all of this playing out as a compelling stage show. The man tastes the invigoration of the bracing air and drinks in majestic vistas—imposing mountain peaks and dramatic sunsets—and fills his lungs with the salt and earthiness of the verdant forest floors.

"I am ecstatic!" he tells his host. "So, this . . . is . . . heaven?"

"No," the angel replies. "I just wanted to make sure you had an opportunity to see all the things you missed while you lived on earth."

In my e-mail inbox today, the subject line seduces: "Balance your life today! An e-workshop opportunity—one time!—for only $389."

How do we see with "new eyes" when it's so easy to be tempted by a quest for solutions to balance our time and, in short, manage our lives? There is comfort in going from A to

B or even from A to Z. Crossing an item off the list is a plea-
sure not easily rivaled for most people. Some of us put things
we've already done on the list, just for the satisfaction of a
check mark.

The real work of sanctuary? To put our burdens down. We
carry a lot around with us, don't we?

- The anxiety of the day
- Past grievances
- Wounds
- An unfair life
- An unpaid debt
- A preoccupation with busyness
- Our desire for perfection
- Self-righteousness
- Our need to impress

Whatever it is, we find reassurance in the weight we carry.
Whatever they are, our burdens prevent us from accepting life
as a gift today.

We are on this journey to name and embrace sanctuaries—places of grace.

I can't repeat this often enough: Sanctuary is not about
management. Or self-improvement. Certainly not about perfection. If we are to seek sanctuary, we have to look for something different from all these ideals. Our seeing has to change
so that our looking can change.

- I don't go to sanctuary to make myself better, because sanctuary is a place where I am at home with my own company.

- I don't go to sanctuary to sort out my life and manage it better, because sanctuary is a place where union is restored, where I receive every part of my life, where I am reconciled with and accepting of my life, however difficult and imperfect.

- I don't go to sanctuary to work or produce because sanctuary is a place of rest.

While I am eager to return to my own sanctuary, my garden, I miss the point entirely if I assume that my sanctuary is a place that I orchestrate or manage. As if the sacred present and tidy control are synonymous.

I spent time recently at a retreat center in the mountains around Tucson, Arizona. Around me was a 360-degree vista of the Tucson, Tortolita, and Santa Catalina mountain ranges. In this desert landscape, the outlines of rock outcroppings are precise and distinct, like a drawing in pen and ink. There are no trees, or at least none compared to where I live, so instead, sand and stone shape the sound of the wind. The Southwest's palo verde tree is unlike our Pacific Northwest trees, which sport great leaves, heedless of a searing summer sun. Our forests are luxuriant and abundant, but here the landscape is minimalist, stripped down. In the Pacific Northwest, our sky and landscape meld, and the treetops look like great slashes of green paint, as if the Creator's hand and broad brush finished the stroke right there. Here in the desert, the colors are muted, distilled to their basic, simple essence.

My heartbeat slows here. The elements conspire to slow me. A part of me wants to know why and figure it all out. Another part of me just accepts the magical elixir of this place, this sanctuary—this reprieve, container, and breathing space. Last night just before dusk, I wandered. I rounded a corner in the path, and there was a stab in my chest at the sight before me. The outcropping of cliff stood in an eerie light. Beyond it, an almost-full moon in a steel-blue sky. In the dusk light, saguaro cactus stood, like grand pincushions or sentinels or long-abandoned maypoles. I took a breath and set down my burdens.

If you try just a little, you will remember a place that offered you this kind of moment. And you'll recall how it changed the way you looked at things. The challenge is how to look at the world differently *every* day. Once we have practiced that for a while, we will find sanctuary more often and in more places, some of them surprising.

But what about life's unsightliness? Can we see heaven there—in the cracks, fault lines, fissures, and suffering that are part of everyday life? I just finished Donald Hall's *The*

Best Day the Worst Day, about life with his wife, Jane Kenyon. Hall writes about the reality of her bipolar disorder and the pain-riddled and complicated last years of Jane's chemotherapy and bone-marrow transplant for leukemia, before her death at age forty-eight.

What I appreciated about Hall's account is the unflinching and meticulous detail to the nuance and fragility (a la Chekhov, who wrote that writers "must illuminate the actual world with a delicate light") of moments, where, if we allow it (even in the middle of fractures and disappointment), beauty walks in and takes residence.

In the book, Hall describes one encounter with a teacher in India, when Hall asked him to define *contentment*.

"Absorbedness," the teacher replied.

Now, I can't find *absorbedness* in any dictionary. But here's my best guess: "Let life in."

- Let life in, in its splendor.
- Let life in, in its complications.
- Let life in, in the disagreeable.
- Let life in, in the unfeigned moments.

As Hall tells us, Jane Kenyon possibly said it best in her final days: "Trust God and be where you are."

On both sides of the equation—whether living as if beauty is only in the magnificent or believing that life's complications interrupt our appreciation of beauty—we assume that we must arrive somewhere else for life to begin. With this mind-set, it is easy to become obsessed and derailed.

In either case, I give my energy to "elsewhere and otherwise," and I miss beauty regardless of where it is found.

I remember talking to a sister—a contemplative woman—about her faith community. She was part of a group of Methodists living in community and following the Rule of St. Benedict. Her insight: "We did it all wrong. And yet, in the end, we did it all right."

I love it. It sounds just like the young man seeking enlightenment, letting go of the need to be perfect.

For years I've lectured and led retreats on sanctuary, many in garden settings. As a garden designer, I'm sometimes asked to re-create a garden to match a photo from a glossy magazine.

"I can," I tell them. "But if I do, you will have a landscape, not a garden. A landscape is for drive-by viewing or public opinion. A garden is to be lived in."

I learned a new word the other day: *sancofa*. From the Akan language of Ghana, it means that it is not wrong to go back and reclaim something that was lost.

I like that; new eyes make it possible to reclaim the fruit of sanctuary: Light, kindness, compassion, understanding, forgiveness, kindheartedness, tolerance, gratitude, mercy, second chances, hope, dignity, open heart, open mind.

During the Bosnian War, Serbs surrounded the city of Sarajevo. The people of Sarajevo knew that sniper fire could kill anyone, whether standing in a bread line or collecting a child from school.

Even so, in the midst of this, Vedran Smailovic brought his cello to play in buildings ruined by the siege. He played in defiance of the madness of war. His music symbolized the indestructibility of the human spirit, despite everything. The music, in essence, became a place of sanctuary for the people of Sarajevo.

In the words of the poet C. P. Cavafy, "We must admit there will be music despite everything."

While I cannot imagine the horror of war, this story—of music and resilience and refuge—strikes a deep chord for me. I want to live in that spirit. I want to be that alive. Even in the midst of anything. Perhaps the cellist in Sarajevo had some internal fortitude most people don't. Isn't that what we think when we witness extraordinary acts of bravery or courage or fearlessness—*it surely cannot exist in me*?

We don't doubt, though, that we know what it is to feel diminished or torn or pulled or overwhelmed or exhausted or belittled. And when we do, we need a place of sanctuary. Because life unravels. We hurt people we love. We take offense. We break or fracture—from sickness, or heartache, or loss. Brokenness can lead us into darkness, and we lose our way.

And it's not just that we lose our way; our life circumstances feel overwhelming, and we feel out of control and—somehow—insufficient.

For this, and many other reasons, we need new eyes. And if it's difficult for us to imagine new eyes, can we at least be willing to think it possible?

Your Sanctuary

- Can you remember looking at an experience or some aspect of your life through a new lens? What changed? How did "looking with new eyes" change the way you grasped or embraced your sense of self?

- What happens when your perspective changes?

- What were the "new" gifts you received from this fresh perspective?

- What is it that makes us hang on to our old ways of seeing?

- It may not be easy to give up the old way (we've always seen it "that way"). Have you ever experienced the freedom of giving up an old way of seeing?

- In what ways have you experienced the freedom of letting the light in with a new perspective?

_____

_____

_____

_____

_____

5

The
Ingredients
of Sanctuary

*The light is what guides you home, the warmth is
what keeps you there.*
—Ellie Rodriguez

"I DON'T HAVE THE MONEY," she tells me. "I love the coast. I love the ocean. I love the rhythm of the waves. They talk to me—yes, I know that sounds weird. But I can sit there and know that I'm not in control of the whole world, and just for a little while I can put down the chunk I've been lugging around." She laughs. "The coast is my sanctuary."

Then she raises her shoulders in a "what can you do?" shrug. "But I can't duplicate that here in a city apartment. And it costs money to get there." Mary lives four hours from the coast. And there is not a lot of time or money for her to enjoy regular visits.

"Who told you you couldn't duplicate it?" I ask. I'm talking with Mary in her apartment, which is a bit disordered, evidence of two adolescent whirlwinds. Mary gives me a look and glances at the scene as if to say, "I rest my case." She's a single mother who works full-time outside the home and has limited income.

Many people go to sacred places—pilgrimages, even visits to the seaside—to be transformed or to lay down a burden or to be surprised. I understand that. But I do believe this: even if we are unable to go physically, we still can go there in our minds. I ask Mary, "What if you had the rhythm of the waves here?"

A week later she calls me. Her voice is animated. "You won't believe this. This is so cool. I was in Goodwill and found a little desktop fountain. I know, I know, it's not the ocean. But I have this new ritual where I take fifteen minutes before the kids get up. I sit in my desk chair, turn off the overhead lights, turn on my little fountain, close my eyes, and I hear the waves."

I'm doing my best to contain my gladness, but I can't. "What?" she asks, hearing my laughter.

"You've honored yourself, and your spirit. And that does my heart good."

Sanctuary takes many forms according to a person's situation, circumstances, needs, and gifts. But there are predictable and recognizable components of sanctuary. They may or may not occur sequentially; however, they are all identifiable and essential—fertile soil for the soul. That's what we'll lay out in this chapter. By the end of it, I hope you'll have a clearer idea of where and how you might create your own sanctuary.

Sanctuary Begins with a Portal

Every sanctuary has its portal, which is a demarcation, an entrance. Portals take you elsewhere—even if only in your mind—and going elsewhere allows you to leave something behind. Remember story time when you were a child? You would settle in, and then the mood would change. As adults, the portal might be physical, such as a gate, archway, or doorway; it might be inside or outdoors. Here are some examples of portals:

- A portal can also exist in time and space, such as a fifteen-minute commute.
- A portal can be the sound of music, chimes, or a rung bell—a trigger changes your focus, like a recess bell at school or a whistle at the end of a factory shift.
- A portal might be a specific room you enter for your sanctuary time.
- A portal might be a garden bench.
- A portal might be a specific area, such as a patio.
- A portal can be a certain point on your walk; when I pass the big oak tree, I know I have entered my sanctuary.

There are also actions that serve as portals when we enter sanctuary:

- An interior portal can be a certain prayer that begins your sanctuary time.
- Perhaps you bless the space, and that blessing is your portal.
- You might have a ceremony of some sort, which includes gestures, postures, words, or actions.
- You might light a candle.

- Your portal may be a mantra, a phrase you repeat for a few moments until you know that you have entered your sanctuary.

We find portals in spiritual practices across cultures and religions. Here are a few, to inspire you and give you an idea or two:

- Noticing small things throughout the day to let you be mindful and aware, such as sitting at a stoplight, hearing a telephone ring, or waiting in line
- Striking a Tibetan singing bowl or a type of bell
- Practicing a breathing exercise, used in various types of yoga and meditation (for example, close your eyes; breathe out three long, slow exhalations; imagine yourself in a familiar room in your home; look around and observe the layout and general color of the room; sense any smells or sounds in the room; breathe out one time; now focus on one object in the room; follow your gaze to this object, seeing the blessings flowing along the beam of your attention; then open your eyes).
- Praying the Office—regular times of prayer throughout the day
- Praying the Native American Circle of Life prayer, which acknowledges that we are connected to all living things

- Saying a *berakah*—a Jewish prayer or blessing, often for "first" things or pleasurable things, such as sunrise, a morning cup of coffee, or a new sighting of a shade of blue in the sky
- Lighting a candle—used in many traditions, including the lighting of the candles during the weeks of Advent or at the beginning of the Jewish Sabbath
- Burning incense, which offers aroma as an invitation to reflection or prayer
- Using rosary beads or other prayer beads to begin a prayer, follow a certain prayer pattern, and then end the prayer
- Using an ordinary object as an anchor or touchstone, a rock, a ring, a wind chime, a coffee mug, to trigger meditations, prayers, or memories

You do have portals. You might not think of them that way, but you have moments when you shift gears and refocus. Can you identify your portal(s)? Can you draw a picture of it/them? There is no magic wand here, just an invitation.

Sanctuary Provides a Container

A sanctuary needs boundaries; otherwise it will fill up with matters not so sanctuary-like. When you're inside your sanctuary, you want to be yourself—creative, prayerful, childlike, unruffled, attentive, hassle-free, playful, detoxified, reclaimed.

And the right container makes a safe place for freedom, expression, reflection, and care.

I know one writer who used plane travel as sanctuary—until in-flight Wi-Fi was introduced; once he transgressed that boundary, the sanctuary ended for him. And he lamented it, wanted it back.

I often present garden talks, and a recent one was "Creating an English Garden in the Pacific Northwest." English gardens are a fusion of wonder and enchantment and magic and abundance. Or, as Vita Sackville-West writes, they are "a sense of profusion within severe lines." That's not such a bad description of our lives.

True, *severe* is a grim adjective—setting the mind in motion and reminding me of my childhood religion when God seemed everlastingly irritated. But Vita is right on. The "severe lines" can make all the difference.

For example, do you know the research about children playing on school playgrounds? At one particular elementary school, there was a big fence around the perimeter, and the students would play using the entire playground, including clambering on this big fence. As the story goes, "child experts" were brought in (someone surely thought, *After all, we can't have all of this clambering*). Their assessment: "The big fence will make the kids feel trapped psychologically, and it needs to be taken down."

Are you ready for this? As soon as the school took down the fence, the kids—instead of playing all over the playground—huddled by the school door. So, the school administration did the right and reasonable thing: They put the fence back up, and the kids felt free to explore the entire area again.

What a wonderful irony: a boundary allows for fearless exploration and freedom.

I often tell people, "Be gentle with yourself." However, we don't cut ourselves much slack, do we? Here's a thought: is it possible that this "boundary" can be *severe mercy*, or mercy that becomes a place for exploration and freedom? Profusion within severe lines indeed.

What are the helpful boundaries of your sanctuary? What kinds of "lines" allow you freedom to explore, to stay open? For example, one of my boundaries is that the sanctuary must be away from my workspace. It also needs to be free of noise.

Sanctuary Slows You Down

I confess that, in my garden design business, I'm not a fan of straight walkways to the front (or back) door. I don't think the walkway needs to be a freeway; it's better if it is designed to slow your steps a bit. Sanctuary is not about speed. The space of sanctuary will slow us down—literally, physically, viscerally. Even in the case of people who jog for their sanctuary—while they are not walking slowly, they are conscious of their breathing. It's good to ask yourself some questions:

- How does this place slow me? Slow my heart, my racing thoughts?
- What elements in this space require me to slow my pace, my breathing, my thoughts?
- Do I have a favorite place to sit? Do I have a favorite chair or bench?
- Is there a vista or pleasant view? Is there a focal point?
- Do I walk? Are there pathways? Do I have a way of walking that causes me to go more slowly so that I can soak in the gifts of this moment and place?

Sanctuary Engages All Our Senses

Joshua Tree National Park has a Junior Ranger program for kids (or the kid in every adult). A program pamphlet provides suggestions and activities. For instance, when visiting a palm oasis, the instructions say:

Visit one of these oases to help you find the answers to the questions below.

- Sit quietly in an oasis for 10 minutes. How does this place make you feel?
- What do you like about it?
- What don't you like?
- What did you notice that surprised you?

Sanctuary grounds us, and often what gives us that grounding is rich and wondrous and demands our utmost attention.

In the Old Testament story, Moses was told, "Take off your shoes, you are on holy ground." I think that means, "Don't let anything get between you and this gift and place of grace."

When I am grounded, I am free to pay attention. Here are some questions about attention:

- What do I notice through seeing? What has changed (the light, the reflections, the sky, the shadows)? What makes me smile?
- What do I hear? We think of some sounds as positive, such as birds chirping. We think of other sounds as negative, such as the persistent noise of traffic. Before we put a moral label on noise, it's okay to invite both kinds of sounds into our sanctuary.
- What do I hear inside my head, mind, and heart? Is the voice there gentle or admonishing and scolding?
- What do I touch? Textures of plants, fabric of a chair, a book I am reading, the wind or breeze in my face, the path under my feet, skin . . .

Here's an exercise I offer to people I'm trying to help reconnect with their senses. It's called a sensory walk. Walk five minutes as rapidly as possible, thinking only of your destination. Focus on nothing else. Just get there. Once you arrive, stop and take at least three deep breaths. Then begin the return journey. This time, walking the same exact path, take at least fifteen minutes. And ask yourself along the way, what do I see? What do I hear? What do I smell, touch, and taste? What is new, surprising, makes me smile, gives me goose bumps? Is there anything I missed along the way?

Sanctuary Is Regular, Specific, and Intentional

Sanctuary doesn't just "happen." Sure, there are times when you happen upon sanctuary. But the sanctuary we need occurs on a regular basis. It is a specific time and place, and we go there intentionally.

We all have preferences and affinities. It's helpful to name them.

- When do I spend time in my sanctuary?
- What time do I prefer for sanctuary? Morning, afternoon, evening?
- How often do I go to sanctuary? Once a week? Once a day?
- What can I give up for the sake of regular and intentional sanctuary time?
- How do I help myself remember sanctuary? Is it on my calendar? Are there alerts on my phone? Is there a person who can help remind me?

Charlie is an artist at heart. He makes his money as a consultant, helping companies develop leaders. We're having dinner at a restaurant, and I ask him, "Do you have a sanctuary?"

"Yes."

I wasn't expecting an immediate response. "Tell me about it."

He thinks and says, "Well, all the words I'm about to use will be wrong." I laugh with him, because that is our knee-jerk response: if we do this sanctuary thing, we have to do it *correctly*.

He describes a small room in his house. ("*My* spot," he tells me.) There he finds peace: "I release the world's stress, my ego takes a day off, I read and sometimes nap, and I'm surrounded by my art projects, which are really parts of my soul."

"What do you read?" I ask.

"I have four books: The Tao, a Celtic prayer book, an English Bible, and a Greek and Hebrew Bible." (I nod, thinking, *I was tracking until you got to the Greek and Hebrew part, but that's a little out of my league*.)

"It's like something is happening in spite of me. The Spirit guides me, talks to me. There's a Celtic practice to paint a white circle, and when you step into that circle for prayer, you are protected. I like that. I feel that way in my room. And sometimes I think about getting a paintbrush and making a circle on the floor." He pauses, "But my wife thinks I'm crazy enough," and laughs.

In Sanctuary, the Inner Critic
Is Turned Off

My grandmother's swing taught me that sanctuary offers the cathartic value of grace.

This is not easy for a gardener. We gardeners suffer this occupational hazard: an inability to sit without noticing weeds. We sit to ponder or reflect or enjoy. And then we spot another blemish to fix. Which leads to updating our "to-do" list and abandoning the garden bench until after we've finished our new projects.

I'm reminded of a comment I overheard: "I want a different kind of life." I understand the sentiment; I just didn't know that life came in *kinds*. With the incessant pressure to live a life other than the one we have, we risk missing out on the very life we long to live.

Do me a favor, would you? Eliminate from your vocabulary this question: "What did you accomplish today?" Whenever anyone asks me, it makes my head spin, and I find myself scrambling for the right sentence just to impress the questioner.

I found myself recently in the garden of Hope Bloesch, a transplanted Australian, walking paths that meandered through profusion. I told the group I was with to give their inner garden critic the day off. It was OK to try at this "gardening with profusion" and really screw up. Why? Because there is no contest here. Gardening is about being present in *this* life. Embracing the present moment can happen while we are observing, drinking in, and enjoying. Times for letting the magic and grace happen.

Some questions are important if you are to create sanctuary that really is just that.

- What allows me to put down my checklist? Is there something physical I do? Is there a prayer or statement I voice?
- Can I mute the phone and put technology in the silent mode?
- Can I enjoy and savor what is still imperfect?
- In this sanctuary space, can I receive as gifts things that are muddled or messy?
- What in this sanctuary not only allows but also encourages me to laugh?

I have a friend who jogs on the path next to Lake Washington "for cardiovascular work," she insists. But she spends a good part of her jog stopped, standing there, just to look at the sky and the clouds. "It's OK," she says. "This is so much better for my heart." How right she is.

A Sanctuary Allows for Self-Nurture

Of course, in creating sanctuary, you have to understand what is nurturing for you—you, not someone else. One person might need music but another silence. One person might be comforted by friendly clutter and another thrives on spare and open spaces.

In my sanctuary, for example, there are objects that connect to my passion or they connect me to my good memories. They bring lightness to my spirit. The questions that follow are not easy or obvious, even for me. I offer them to you and to myself at the same time:

- What brings lightness to your spirit?
- What do you find healing?
- What frees you?
- What makes you feel most alive? When do you feel especially glad to be alive?

I live on an island in the Puget Sound. A ferry is our only mode of travel on or off the Rock (as we affectionately call it). If you're in a hurry, you won't last long here. You'll race for a boat. Or you'll miss a boat. And you won't have a book in your car to keep you company for the one-hour wait until the next ferry.

I moved here from the bustle of Southern California, from freeway gridlock to an island without a stoplight. The move wasn't an answer to some lack in my life, because I wasn't sure what I was missing.

Today, I am a writer, a gardener, and a pilgrim. But not necessarily in that order. And I must confess to you that as pilgrims go, I'm of a most improper sort.

Don't for a minute think that I have given up "preaching the word." It's just that now my pulpit is an old bench under the plum tree, where I'm fortified by the bracing scent of a honeysuckle vine. The pews are patches of dandelion-filled lawn off to the side of the wood fence on which the honeysuckle climbs. A trio of Swainson's thrush forms our choir. It is Sacrament Sunday. But then every day is Sacrament Sunday. The sermon today is "Cultivating the Good Life by Embracing the Art of Doing Nothing."

I have a friend who gives me grief for what he calls my "sell all and flee to the country" sermon. There's no doubt, I do feel the need to leave the hustle and bustle. And I'll be the first to admit that moving for the sake of moving is not the answer, either. There is certainly no formula here. But I dare you to sit on this bench with me, long enough to let the honeysuckle warm your blood and soothe your spirit and reconnect you with something fundamental and sacred.

Before you know it, the passion for self-nurture takes root. It's only a matter of time.

Sanctuary Offers Refuge

On the radio program *A Prairie Home Companion*, Garrison Keillor tells a poignant story about the fictitious Lake Wobegon life on the northern Minnesota prairie, where children knew what it meant to travel a great distance to school. And where a sudden winter storm is life threatening.

In preparation for a winter storm emergency, each child is assigned a storm home, a place nearer the school, where the child will go, and stay, if the weather becomes too treacherous for travel. On the first day of school, slips of paper are given to each child. The paper says: "Your storm home is with the _____ (blank) family."

Garrison tells of being assigned to the Krugers. The Krugers were an elderly couple and, as he recalls, very kindly. They had an impeccable house with a fence around a large yard. On normal school days Garrison would walk by the house and imagine what it would be like if he had to take refuge there. He imagines the crackling fireplace, a delicious meatloaf, and a quilt on the bed. And Garrison imagines Mr. Kruger speaking to the principal, and pointing over toward him and saying, "There, that little boy over there—we would like him for our storm child." All of this imagining made Garrison feel secure, even though, as it happened that school year, he never had to stay in his storm home.

Even so. Sometimes every one of us needs a storm home.

Not so long ago, for several days in the Pacific Northwest, we couldn't go anywhere. The ground was covered with snow, which was covered by a sheet of ice and dusted with more snow. The forecast called for freezing rain. When the governor of the state tells you to "stay indoors," that's serious. Although, if you are so inclined, some of the side roads are perfect for cross-country skiing, especially without any traffic.

I spent two of those days (with half of the city of Seattle) at Sea-Tac Airport, our schedules recalibrated and plans scuttled. I passed some of the time reliving the memories and stories of another big storm from 2008, when we were housebound for days.

Every big storm on the island I live on breaks a record of sorts—making it a "real storm" here in the Northwest. The day before a "real storm," all islanders (unaccustomed to snow of any kind) hightailed it to the supermarket (the store a frenzy of anxiety, with shoppers cramming their carts with jugs of drinking water, batteries, candles, and a bottle or two of Syrah. Let's face it, there's no sense riding out any storm without some fine Syrah).

Our driveway was impassable, the main roads iced and precarious, and nothing on the day's agenda was worth taking a risk. Such days are made for sitting inside and looking out. On our patio sits a great chocolate-brown terra-cotta pot, home to a Russian olive tree. The tree was bowed, deferential, and weighted with snow. From where I sat, the pot looked like a perfect cupcake, frosted with over a foot of meringue.

The woodlands were silent. Outside our windows, it was a white winter framed with shadowed trees, a still-life painting in black and white, unspoiled and ageless. The snow blanketed the trees and shrubs and the stalks of spent perennials. On a nearby rosebush, I saw two bubblegum-pink rosebuds still tight-fisted. Though stooped in the snow, they were a picture of optimism.

The entire landscape allowed a space for pausing, waiting, exhaling.

When sanctuary happens—sometimes unexpectedly—there is no work to be done. In the garden, it is time for the ground to lie fallow. That day, and others like it, I spent time in my storm home.

Not all storms are weather related. Life bears storms of its own. Grief perhaps (a church leader whom I respected and admired died this week, and I am very sad), or conflict (I couldn't quite see eye-to-eye on a project dispute, and it was difficult to avoid hard feelings), or melancholy (call it what you want, but there are days when we carry a sadness or heaviness for reasons we cannot explain). Too often, we try to weather the storm on our own; we don't even want a storm home.

But having a storm home makes a difference. It is another way of knowing, "I am held safe here."

As you reflect on your own sanctuary, think about it as a storm home. How will it hold up during those hard, blustery times? Do you have what you need there?

Sanctuary Renders Healing

There are moments in our lives that can change everything.

For Chris Orwig, it happened in a tent at the base of the Sierra Nevada mountain range in California. He was camping with a group of friends. When his friends first invited him, Chris said no. He relented when they told him they would "car camp" the first night. *I can do that*, Chris told himself.

You see, Chris experienced constant pain throughout his entire body. Walking was *never* easy. Climbing a mountain, *impossible*, he thought.

When the debilitating pain began during Chris's early twenties, various medical experts had no answers. "I couldn't do most of the things I enjoyed doing." With that realization, Chris hit bottom. "I was completely broken. I was cracked. I was undone. Because I defined myself by what I could and couldn't do."

His first reaction when invited to climb a mountain? "Here's another thing I *can't* do." To Chris, life had become impassable. Have you ever felt that way? I can tell you that I have.

But there's good news. We never know when we will find or receive or take hold of hope.

"My father gave me a camera," Chris tells me. (*OK*, his father was saying, *so you can't surf anymore, but you can still take pictures of something you love.*) That camera became Chris's passport to exploration. It also became his portal to sanctuary. "It did something to me." Instead of allowing himself to focus on the pain, the camera transported him into the larger world.

Chris recalls a day when he saw a palm tree, an ordinary California palm tree. Except that this palm tree was growing from a street gutter, against all odds, stretching for the light. *That*, he told himself, *is what I want to be, in a world no longer defined by the label of what I can't or shouldn't be.*

With camera in hand, Chris says, "My healing began." There is beauty to behold everywhere, and all art requires a fight, an intentional choice to see beauty, or not.

Back in the tent on that first morning, Chris woke up alone and in the dark. He thought, *They will climb the mountain today, and I will be left behind.* There was a gap in the tent. He could see the stars and watched as the dawn delivered daylight, and soon after, the vista of mountains.

What he hears from his friends he does not expect, "Let's go, Chris. You're coming with us." They have fashioned a contraption with a lawn chair on poles using duct tape. On the way up the mountain, they would pass by other hikers, and he would wave, referring to himself as the Pharaoh of the John Muir Trail. It takes courage to pray for a miracle. It takes more courage to receive that miracle in the form of a lawn chair.

Life can be too big sometimes. And we all have been broken, cracked, undone. We have all felt that we can't do or be.

With any limitation or disease, I'm hoping there is a lesson to be learned to ease the pain. And if I'm lucky, a miracle to right the wrong. But what if *having the answer* is not the point? Sometimes when we ask for "the answer" what we really want is an explanation; we're hoping to fit life and limitations into categories we can more easily understand. But do explanations really heal us?

In the Gospel of John, Jesus encounters a man who has been lying on a mat, with a disability, for thirty-eight years.

He's been waiting that long to be healed. Jesus asks him a simple question, "Do you *want* to get well?"

In Chris's case, "Will you choose to see life through the lens of a camera?"

Dr. Sherwin Nuland once wrote: "There is a big difference between what we call *disease* and what we call *illness*. A disease is a pathological entity; an illness is the effect of the disease on the patient's entire way of life." Healing is deeper than changing our limitations, physical or emotional. We heal when we give ourselves permission to embrace the sacred in each moment. Hope sees the sacred in the ordinary moments of every day, even in those moments that may break our hearts. Awareness leads us to embrace life as it is, with all its challenges and risks, to see beauty and wonder regardless of the vessel.

I'm headed back out to the garden, my sanctuary:

- I go to my garden to let the cares of the day dissipate.
- I go to my garden to listen to my heart.
- I go to my garden to regain my soul.
- I go to my garden to hear the voice of grace.

Your Sanctuary

Assess your spaces and places: home, workplace, play place, worship space, the places where you spend free time.

Ask yourself these questions:

- Where do I feel safe? What gives me a sense of safety?
- When I'm in this space, what happens inside me? What happens in my mind, my spirit, my heart?
- Does this space help me feel unhurried? Does it help me settle?
- Does this space allow for quiet or stillness?
- In which of these spaces is my mind free to meander, to ponder, to laugh, to contemplate, to think outside the box?
- Is there a particular space that seems the most like sanctuary? What aspects of sanctuary are present there?

For your "portal," here's a ritual you might try:

1. Ask God for light that you might see the day.
2. Express gratitude for the gift of this day.
3. Look back over the events of the day.
4. When were you most aware of sacred presence?
5. When were you least aware and why?
6. Choose one part of the day to pray for.
7. What do you look forward to for tomorrow?

6

Hurdles on the Way to Sanctuary

ELLEN, A WRITER, IS RECENTLY WIDOWED. Her new book about the grief process is written in the first person for a good reason: Ellen understands grief.

Ellen is also a spiritual director, familiar with the language of spiritual growth and development. She knows how to tell people about taking care of their inner life. But she also knows that those who teach don't always practice what they teach. I think it's because it's hard to give yourself permission for self-care.

Her husband's illness dragged on, and Ellen was his full-time caregiver. No one is ever ready to take on the weight of such an obligation, no matter our makeup, training, or internal reserves.

People said to Ellen: "You need time off. You need rest. You need replenishing."

"It's odd," she tells me, "to look in the mirror and realize that a voice tells you that you don't deserve time off."

Most of us will say, with little hesitance, that we need sanctuary. But on our way to experience sanctuary, a lot can happen. A few things might even get in the way, like big hurdles on what we'd prefer was a nice, smooth track. Probably every person has his or her particular kind of hurdle—I can't give you an exhaustive list. But your troubles on the way to sanctuary might fit into one of these categories:

- Logistical challenges, such as not having the right time or place
- Too much caution and fear
- You're sure you'll be doing it wrong
- Cages and restrictions we might not even see
- Stuckness, or negative self-talk, an inability to move away from harmful beliefs about yourself

Logistical Challenges

Marjory does her best most days to find a smile. She is a cancer survivor, which is good news, but she is young, still in her twenties, and the mother to a beautiful eighteen-month-old daughter. To say life can be heavy is an understatement. There is no father in the picture; he left long ago. Marjory's mother is nearby and helps with child care when she can. Marjory works a part-time job and is committed to making a life for her little princess. Fighting cancer and life's burdens is enough, so how does she find the time or the space (in a very small apartment), let alone the energy, for the things that give us hope and release?

"I don't have any place," Marjory tells me. "My life is overwhelming, I'm still anxious about my health. And I want my daughter to have a life. And not just a sick mom."

I am visiting Marjory, filming her for a segment for the Hallmark TV show *New Morning*.

"What if I helped?" I ask.

"OK." I can tell by her tone that she's skeptical.

While small, her apartment does have a balcony, with enough space for a small table and a chair or two. "Do you use it?" I ask.

"When would I have the time? And besides, what's to see—other than our lovely parking lot?" She laughs.

"Let's go," I say, and we head to a local nursery—any nursery will do.

"It's your patio. What do you want?"

"Anything?" We walk the aisles and fill a cart with a dozen plants, including an Asiatic lily that reminds her of her grandmother. Back at the apartment, we go to work. We put a tablecloth on the table. A plant sits with a candle. In the corner of the balcony, a lily and a very tall fern. I admit, I'm having fun. We're on the patio. Marjory is getting teary-eyed, and she tells me why: "I didn't think I deserved this."

"Will you use it today?"

"My mother watches my little girl on Tuesdays. I'll make it my patio morning. I love to write but haven't given myself time."

She adjusts the scarf on her head, smiles, and realizes that she is standing in her sanctuary. And it's all her own.

We can't deny that logistical challenges exist in our lives. But we can learn to look at the situation and see possibilities we may not have noticed before. For Marjory it was a patio she had disregarded. For you, it may be a schedule that's too full—one that might have some flexibility if you are willing to make a choice or two. The point is, don't just name your physical limitations.

Take a chance and ask some questions: *What am I overlooking? Is there another way to think about this? What are the possibilities here?* You wouldn't be the first person to discover that a certain walk-in closet could be emptied of stuff you didn't actually use—and transformed into a little space big enough to dream in.

Too Much Caution and Fear

I remember a walk along the shore of Lake Michigan, on the campus of Northwestern University, our backdrop the straight-edge line of a powder-blue horizon toward the east and the Chicago skyline to the south. My friend and I had nowhere to go, and we weren't in a hurry to get there. It seemed a good day for a long and restful nothing.

At the entrance to an inviting tree-dotted and grassy area, a prominently placed sign greets all who walk into this place of respite, rest, and sanctuary: "Enter at your own risk."

I had to do a double take. And I laughed. But then it made me sad. At one level, everything now in our world is tainted with the fear of liability. After all, someone might get hurt. (Although it doesn't read well on your medical report, "Injuries sustained while loitering.") So, risk becomes a double-edged sword. However, I believe that in our fear-tinged world, we give our energy to casting a watchful eye over the danger always lurking (or the enemies always at bay). We live tense and on edge.

Be careful! You could be injured, frightened, attacked, alarmed, or—worse—sued. And our lives are now predicated on limiting liability. Isn't it interesting what happens when we choose (or live by) that particular choice of words, "be careful"? When I "enter at my own risk," I instinctively perceive my experience in a narrower or more restrictive framework. I live in that moment anticipating fear.

So it's not just about caution. Yes, I understand that there are times when caution is called for. What troubles me is that more often than not, I trade in my freedom or imagination or choice or intention or unabashed delight or even my contentment, because I am certain I may offend or that I don't deserve it, or that I haven't earned it, or that I have colored outside the lines, and must pay the price. Sort of like that faithful band of "believers" in the movie *Babette's Feast*, who, when offered an extraordinarily generous gift of the feast of a lifetime, make the decision to "taste" the wine, but not "enjoy it."

I read a story about a neighborhood near San Diego, California, where, fifteen years ago, children climbed trees, built forts, floated homemade boats in the stream, fished for bluegill in the little pond near the public library, and savored their days in a community cherished for its "open space"—a community that boasted on its welcome sign, "Country Living." And then, it all stopped. "Authoritative adults" from the community organization intervened. "Somehow," resident John Ricks reported, "the tree house was now a fire hazard, and the 'dam' the children created in the small stream might cause severe flooding."

So the children adapted. They moved their "play" space from the woodland to the asphalt. Families erected basketball hoops in driveways, and kids created ramps for skateboards on the sidewalks.

And the community association reminded the residents that such activities violated the covenants they had signed when they bought their houses. So down came the ramps and poles, and inside went the kids—to their video games and screen time.

Yes, we need to make choices regarding safety. But our idea of safety has changed a lot, driven by fear. I don't want to see kids live that way—and I don't want to live in fear either.

The fact is, a life worth living has its share of risk. To really care, grieve, love, begin again, give birth to passion, open your heart, accept loss, be overcome by beauty, sustain friendship, sit in stillness, wrestle with prayer and faith, tell the truth, and offer sanctuary to sadness or joy requires a heart willing to accept risk and be broken—to be broken wide open.

The truth is that if I do enter a place of sanctuary, or if I do honor stillness, or if I do give up my diversions to be at home in my own skin, or if I do choose the courage to be fully present, it might not be easy. It might, in fact, be risky.

This is the great irony: "enter at your own risk" need not mean "shut down your heart" or restrict your life or your passion or your sorrow or your joy. It is the opposite: "enter at your own risk" precisely because your heart is fully engaged, fully alive.

Cages and Restrictions We Might Not Even See

Mohini was a regal white tiger. In the 1960s and 1970s, she lived at the National Zoo in Washington, DC. Most of those years she lived in the old lion house, a twelve-by-twelve-foot cage with iron bars and a cement floor. Mohini spent her days pacing restlessly back and forth in her cramped quarters while zoo visitors watched, pointing in awe.

Eventually, biologists and staff worked to move Mohini from such an artificial and cramped environment to a more natural and suitable habitat for her. Mohini's new home covered several acres, with hills, trees, a pond, and a variety of vegetation. With excitement and anticipation, they released Mohini into her new and spacious environment.

No one expected what occurred next.

Instead of frolicking in newfound freedom, Mohini immediately sought refuge in a corner of the compound, where she lived for the remainder of her life. Mohini paced and paced in that corner until, in the end, it made a twelve-by-twelve-foot area, worn bare of grass.

Why wouldn't Mohini have treasured her new space? After I read Mohini's story I had an immediate response, which included a litany of how we too easily live too-small lives. But it's not that simple, is it? I haven't always seen the cages around me, and I've had a grocery list of "guidance" that threw all sorts of unhelpful cages around me: "Do you know what your problem is?" "Are you crazy? You can't do that." "Well, of course. Can't you see?! If only you would . . ." Usually we don't need help understanding that we need to change, but it doesn't help to have well-intentioned (or worse, self-righteous) people add to the cages we've already allowed to be placed there. Some of the more popular of these cages: "I have to do more to be okay" and "I am somehow incomplete." These types of statements only reinforce the belief that our life is elsewhere and otherwise, and assuredly, not possible where it is *now*.

We may want to love other people without holding back. We may want to feel authentic. We may want to breathe in the beauty around us. We may want to dance and sing. And yet each day we listen to inner voices that keep life small. We are in a cage of sorts. We tell ourselves, *Don't. I shouldn't. It can't be done. What am I thinking? I know that won't work, don't I?*

Perhaps one of the biggest tragedies in our lives is that freedom is possible, yet we pass our years trapped in the same old patterns. Entangled in some kind of trance—scripts about unworthiness or marginalization or shame or powerlessness or inadequacy. Our self-judgment and anxiety become our very own cage. We spend our days in restlessness and dissatisfaction. And we end up just like Mohini, pacing in the corner of our domain; we grow incapable of accessing the freedom and peace that are our birthright.

And it's not the external boundaries that make a difference; it's the internal ones. This is where we go a bit offtrack. You see, believing our boundaries are external, we seek an external solution—say a whole new environment with hills and a pond and such (or perhaps the addition of a new BMW convertible, just saying).

Perhaps we can try a new affirmation:

> If I assume my identity is confined to a cage,
> I will carry that identity with me wherever I go.
> However, when I learn that my identity is deeper
> —more profound and remarkable—
> and that I am loved and cherished regardless of any cage,
> then, the iron bars begin to disappear.

We can learn to live from strength, not limitation.

Stuckness: The Inability to Move Away from Harmful Beliefs about Ourselves

There are many different variations on feeling stuck. Whether we feel immobilized or powerless or incapable or simply frozen, we are stuck.

My friend has a passion but finds herself in a job she loathes. "I cry from my house to my car every day," she says. "And all this negativity just pervades my whole life." Truth is, I

have known that feeling: *I don't want to be here. I'm not myself.*
Feeling squeezed, claustrophobic, out of control and worse,
sorry for myself. We are stuck when we believe any of these
things:

- I am not enough.
- I am small and not gifted.
- I am carried by the winds of public opinion.
- My identity is tied to shame.
- I owe it to someone to be perfect.
- I am at the mercy of my own grief or rage.

The irony here, of course, is that we try to solve the problem
of being stuck—of being out of balance or constricted—by
adding even more pressure to ourselves, in order to become
unstuck. We enroll in balance seminars, take balance classes,
and buy balance apps for our smartphones. All of this serves
only to keep us from being fully alive or authentic. So maybe
the way we put an end to the gnawing effect of fear and insuf-
ficiency is that instead of bravely ignoring these experiences (or
pushing past them), we find, in the depths of them, the heart
of mercy and compassion we can share with all life. It's the
same heart of mercy and compassion that some great spiritual
leaders have called the divine essence. At the end of the day,
that essence is not interested in whether you "made it" but in
what you became and what became of you along the way.

You may have heard the story about the man who prayed, "Dear God, today I want to win the lottery." This he prayed, every day.

But he didn't win. Weeks went by. Months went by.

Finally, in desperation he prayed, "God, I've prayed to you. I've pleaded with you. Why will you not grant my wish? I want to win the lottery."

And God answered him, "If I were you, I'd buy a ticket."

I don't know how to promise you to become unstuck. So here's my recommendation: this week, buy a ticket, but a ticket to live front and center in *this* life, in this moment, to waste more time, to be curious, to wonder, to ask, to gawk, to savor, to grin, to point, to notice. And when you talk with God, use your hands (don't worry, people will think you're talking on a Bluetooth). Daydream, journal, stare, linger, amble, give, receive, pay attention, meander, count clouds, make up new names for colors (melancholy blue, grandmother's-hug blue), compliment someone, pet dogs, kiss babies, go into bakeries just to smell the air.

Your Sanctuary

What keeps you stuck?

What messages did you receive when you were younger that told you that you weren't enough, or didn't have what it took to embrace a life that nurtured the self and the soul?

Which of these hurdles gives you the most discontent or dissatisfaction, lack of time, lack of privacy, lack of a serene space, lack of confidence, fear of blunders?

What is there about our culture that gives so much energy to what can *get in the way,* to what can *go wrong?* Do you ever hear yourself say, "I can't do that because . . ."

To overcome an obstacle, what might you need? Help from a friend? Permission to try and fail? To hear an inspirational story about someone who overcame obstacles?

_____

_____

_____

_____

_____

_____

_____

_____

_____

_____

_____

_____

_____

_____

_____

_____

_____

_____

_____

_____

_____

_____

_____

7

Sanctuary with and for Others

THERE IS ENOUGH PAIN TO GO AROUND. Sometimes it's personal. Call it loneliness or sadness or cheerlessness. And sometimes we see it in others around us. And we want to help but don't know how. Or what do we say? I guess we're wired to want to fix people and solve whatever it is that muddles their world.

Patsy Swendson has a big heart. She's also a dog lover. Those two qualities kind of go together. A few years ago, when our young men and women were returning home from wars—Iraq and Afghanistan—there was nothing to prepare their caregivers, whether it be hospital workers or family or friends. Most of the returnees came home the worse for wear. They'd seen a lot. Their hearts hurt. And their bodies were not the same, many of them permanently damaged, many missing limbs.

Patsy visited the VA hospital's polytrauma unit. And she took with her a friend, Kelsey, her golden retriever and lab mix. By her own admission, Patsy wasn't sure what to say or do. What would she find there? What would she witness?

What would be needed from her? How could she meet the needs of people so wounded? Was there a list of some sort, instructions? She knew two things: These young people could use a friend. And a four-footed furry being could turn a life around, bring order out of chaos, bring love and hope to a person who has none.

Patsy told me many stories about the VA. I especially remember one about Trevor, who had three limbs amputated.

"He looked up at me blankly. I smiled, 'Good morning. Do you want a visit from a cute blonde?'" He nodded that it would be OK.

Kelsey stood by the bed, her face looking up. With his remaining arm, Trevor instinctively scratched the dog's ears.

"She can snuggle up to you, and she won't hurt you. Would that be OK?" He nodded. Kelsey is now on the bed, with her head on the stump of the young man's leg.

Trevor had no words, just tears.

"Are you OK?" Patsy asked.

"It's the first time anyone wanted to touch me. And the first time in a long time that I've felt warm. And loved."

We are on this journey to name and embrace sanctuaries—places of grace. Along this journey, some of us have named our sanctuaries. Some of us have discovered a place that has been there all along.

And some of us know how easy it is to forget or to allow the tide of life—busyness, obligations, misfortune, pain—to hide our sanctuary from us. In these times we need to help others create the sanctuary they need and offer help when they feel they cannot create or find it on their own.

In war, the young men and women spent their days with "battle buddies," people who had their back. Now here at home, sometimes all alone, their battle buddy is a furry creature who quite literally never leaves their side, thanks to Patsy Swendson and her therapy-dog organization.

When we make space we are able to bring who we are—whether we are grieving or sad or bewildered or overflowing with joy and gratitude.

Beth Campbell started the Buddy Ball program in 1994, in Bellevue, Washington. Because of his disabilities, Beth's seven-year-old son Stevie was unable to play in the local T-ball program. So Beth started a baseball league that partners able-bodied children with children who have disabilities. Every player has a buddy, and every team has eighteen players. It works like this:

- If you can't hit, a buddy hits for you.
- If you can't throw, a buddy throws for you.
- If you can't run, a buddy runs for you.
- If you can't catch, a buddy catches for you.
- If you're in a wheelchair, a buddy pushes you around the bases.

At the Buddy Ball games, you will see unmitigated joy on the faces of children who may never be able to catch a fly ball but who *know* that they are playing in the game, on a team.

And here's something else you should know about Buddy Ball: It is against the rules to strike out. Once you get six strikes, you get to go to first base. You are rewarded for trying. That's all about grace.

But such grace unnerves some people. At a conference for professionals, I told the Buddy Ball story. After my lecture, a therapist literally was in my face, letting me know where I went amiss. "Six strikes and you still get to go to first. How dare you teach that kind of freedom to children!" his face was puffed and red. "Sir," I said, "with all due respect, you could use more roughage in your diet."

I'm paraphrasing now, from an article in the *Seattle Times*: "When Beth's son gets to first base, he doesn't stop there. But he doesn't go to second either. He runs out into the crowd and hugs everybody."

The reporter continued: "It is what sports can be, children running and jumping and playing because nobody's keeping score because nobody cares."

Sanctuary is—after all the preaching is done—about liberation. And freedom. And grace. I know this now. Instead of preaching a sermon, many times it would have been more appropriate if I had dismissed the service and told the congregation to run out into the crowds of their day and hug everybody.

I had a weekend to work in my garden. Our tulip bulbs—lavender and butter yellow—are about to flower. We covered all the garden beds with manure, an annual and sacred liturgy. I transplanted blueberry shrubs. I mourned the loss of all my Mediterranean-style plants (who met their fate in this past very cold, wet Seattle winter) and said a eulogy at the compost heap. And I sat on my back deck and talked with the pair of mallard ducks who call our pond their home.

And I thought of Buddy Ball and hoped that every person who reads this book will go hug somebody and feel hugged in return.

Your Sanctuary

Some questions to ponder and/or journal about:

It's easier to see when others are overwhelmed than it is to see ourselves overwhelmed in our own life. And we can recognize times when we provide sanctuary—a safe place of grace—for another. Why is it so difficult to receive that gift from others?

Have you ever been in a place in your life where you needed someone to provide sanctuary for you?

When someone has been a sanctuary for you, what did they provide in terms of qualities, environment, specific ingredients?

Think of the people in your life. Do you know anyone who could use sanctuary? What would sanctuary look like for them? How could you help make that happen?

_____

_____

_____

_____

_____

_____

_____

8

Creating
Sanctuary in
Public Places

I was preparing to give a talk and had a very different story planned, but a walk in the park changed my mind.

Yesterday I walked—strolled and ambled—the length of Central Park in New York. The day was sunny and warm, in the high fifties, virtually summer temperatures for the east coast this year. And it appeared that the whole of Manhattan had the same idea: *Let's go to the park. We can breathe there.* It was as if there had been some kind of mass migration from hibernation, spilling from the high-rises that frame the park.

I didn't walk far before a bench beckoned to me. The sun was a sedative, an intoxicating tonic that soothed my disquiet and settled the nerves.

On a post nearby I saw a sign: "The Great Lawn. Closed for the season to rest." I smiled, thinking that it wouldn't be a bad idea if we hung a smaller version of that sign around our necks every now and again. The park was white, still blanketed in snow but, in the sunlight, alive with possibility.

The world orbited by—parents with strollers, moms, dads, couples, tourists, lifelong New Yorkers, dog lovers, and a virtual marathon of joggers. Even though cell phones are ubiquitous, on this day, no one passing me by had found the need to talk on one. On this day there was no need for distraction. So the phones served their ancillary purpose as journaling devices, documenting the moments, the smiles, the vistas, the goodwill.

There was something about the light, I thought, as I relished the warmth on my face. It was an invitation to explore, saunter, sit, savor, grin (for no real reason), soak up oomph, point, laugh out loud, and refuel.

And then my mind wandered to that inescapable list and litany of things left undone.

I had received several e-mails that week from people asking for counsel or for me to lend an ear. They needed company while they ruminated on life's vicissitudes: exhaustion and disappointment and grief and sadness (and in some cases all four). I was glad for those e-mails, because I know what it means to wrestle with discontent, and I wanted to be helpful. I also wanted to be insightful, to find the precise words that would comfort and uplift (as if my words of compassion were to be judged like an Olympic event: "Very nice—6.5 on empathy!")

But now, in the park, I watched a young boy eagerly telling his parents where he wanted to go and what he wanted to see. His enthusiasm stirred me from my own thoughts, and I saw the joy on his face, which reminded me that life is not a race or a contest or a beauty pageant. It is a gift—pure and simple.

I design gardens. Many are private gardens, but I also design public spaces. Not long ago I spent a weekend with a church. Fifty of its members had gathered to talk about creating "sanctuary space" around their church. I told them that their designs must begin with this assumption: Worship (devotion or reverence) or Liturgy is not what happens after you enter the front door. Worship begins when you enter the property.

"Wait a minute," one was bold enough to interject. "You're talking about our landscaping?"

"No," I answered. "I'm talking about creating intentional spaces where sanctuary is real. We don't enter this space only because it's beautiful. We don't enter this space only because it's useful. We enter this space because we need to connect with grace."

The church committee's temptation was understandable. "What are the *rules* for creating this public space?" they asked me. I told them in response about a story I had heard about Rear Admiral Thornton Miller, the chief chaplain at Normandy during World War II. Someone asked him, "Up and down the beach, with the shells going everywhere, why did you go to the wounded soldiers?"

"Because I'm a minister."

"But didn't you ask if they were Catholic or Protestant or Jew?"

"If you're a minister, the only question you ask is, 'Can I help you?'"

What we too often fail to see is that *we* are the gift. We carry the divine spark, the image of our Creator.

A rather unsophisticated man endured a medical operation with a 20 percent chance of survival. When told about his condition and the odds that were against him, he engaged in no calculations and did not consult with another physician. He said simply, "I want to be one of the 20 percent."

One year later, he reduced his work hours to make the time to travel several miles for radiation treatment, asking about an increased dosage in order to "heal faster." Intrigued by the man's capacity to take charge and his persistent drive in the midst of a toxic environment—including the cacophony of expertise issuing from all sorts of people, some more helpful than others—his therapist, Dr. Edwin Friedman, wondered how the man did it.

In a session with the man, Dr. Friedman told a story about the USS *Indianapolis*. At fourteen minutes past midnight, on July 30, 1945, midway between Guam and Leyte Gulf, two torpedoes from a Japanese submarine hit the ship. Nine hundred men were left helpless in the hostile environment of the Japan Sea, enduring shark attacks, potential starvation, terrible thirst, and suffering from exposure and their wounds. Although they knew it was to their advantage to stay close to one another (there were no lifeboats), some of the men swam away from the safety of the group and, willingly or out of desperation, gave themselves up to the sharks.

"How do you explain that?" Dr. Friedman asked his client. "Unless you assume they were exhibiting extraordinary altruism, those men who swam away functioned in exactly the opposite direction from the one you have followed with regard to the dangers to your own life. And yet, you have responded with cool, with stamina, with perspective, and with courage."

The man answered quickly, "Those guys who swam away, they didn't have no future."

We are not in shark-infested waters, although some days it might feel that way, because of cruel luck or, in my case this week, the loss of a loved one. Which way should we swim? Which way should we turn? Why do some of us make it, and some of us don't?

There is a notion that the people who make it—those who have stamina, perspective, and courage—are not the norm. They must be exceptional for that very reason. We might think they have a certain brand of willpower or an inside connection to God or miraculous luck. Lord knows there are enough tragic cases of heartbreaking luck.

This is where we go amiss with our mental gymnastics. To have a future is not about eternity or even about our golden years. It is about the permission, the freedom, and the persistence to *love* this very day. And so often, a sanctuary allows us that permission. It may be Central Park on a glorious afternoon. It may be a community of people who accept you just as you are.

In his book *Crossing the Unknown Sea*, David Whyte talks about exhaustion. He asked his spiritual director for help. He was told, "The antidote to exhaustion is wholeheartedness."

"Excuse me?"

"You are so tired through and through because a good half of what you do here has nothing to do with your true powers.

You are only half here; half here will kill you after a while. You need something to which you can give your full powers."

On a June day in 1944, two weeks after D-Day, a few miles from the bloody shores of Omaha Beach, members of the 404th Fighter Group worked to carve an airstrip out of the Normandy countryside. Their efforts resulted in the loss of twenty-eight army engineers at the hands of the German snipers who persisted and fought after the D-Day battle. Most were located and captured or killed. One lone sniper still remained in the nighttime distance.

Back at the airstrip, Captain Jack Tueller took out his trumpet. He'd used it on many a starlit night to entertain the men of the 508th. His commander told him, "Not tonight. I know your trumpet makes the most glorious sound, but with the sniper still out there, you will put us in harm's way."

In Tueller's own words, "I thought to myself, that German sniper is as lonely and scared as I am. How can I stop him from firing? So I played the German love song, 'Lili Marleen' [made famous in the late '30s by Marlene Dietrich, the legendary German actress]. And I wailed that trumpet over those apple orchards of Normandy. And he didn't fire."

The next morning, the military police approached Tueller to tell him they had a German prisoner on the beach who kept asking, "Who played that trumpet last night?"

Tueller describes the moment: "I grabbed my trumpet and went down to the beach. There was a nineteen-year-old German boy, scared and lonesome. He was dressed like a French peasant to cloak his role as a sniper. And, crying, he said, 'I couldn't fire because I thought of my fiancée. I thought of my mother and father. My role is finished.'"

"He stuck out his hand, and I shook the hand of the enemy," Tueller said. "[But] he was no enemy, because music had soothed the savage beast."

I love this story because music unlocks mercy, and who knows, maybe even the possibility for forgiveness or healing.

Every one of us is afraid at times. Who knows all the reasons. But when it happens we revert to a *zero-sum view* of the world. Resources—including compassion, mercy, kindness, and generosity—are finite. Life is short, and you get what you can. And if I don't know you, you are my enemy, or at the very least, someone to be mistrusted.

This week I was charmed by a story about a woman named Sarah, an ordinary woman with a peculiar habit. You see, every Saturday, when the Jehovah's Witnesses made their neighborhood rounds, she invited them in. She begins by saying to them, "I'm glad to see you. I'm not going to convert, but you all are welcome to stay for tea." And every Saturday, the visitors did just that.

Another time, a salesman dropped in—an old-fashioned door-to-door vacuum-cleaner salesman. "Come on in," she told him. "I need to tell you that I'm not going to buy, and my baby is asleep, so no loud demo, but you look like you've had a long day. Would you like a cup of coffee?"

"Why?" the salesman asked.

"Well, this may sound strange, but I actually believe that God may be found in any person, so I'm offering you coffee because you might be Jesus."

I'm certain that for the salesman, it was easily his strangest house call ever, but he sat for a spell and enjoyed the coffee.

There was a time where I would have overlooked this story or would have dismissed it. It falls under the category of "too good to be true or possibly crazy." We live in a world where, because of fear, we mistrust just about everyone and everything. Even kindness, and especially kindness. But this is not a story about kindness. Sarah made a little sanctuary, that's all.

When we create sanctuaries, we are creating places of healing. We are making space to see and to be seen. To give wholeheartedly. To offer comfort or reprieve or hope. To "do sanctuary" in a world of disquiet, disruption, and misgiving. To welcome—or invite—others who need the reminder: "Come on in." Maybe that is what we need. One cup of tea or coffee at a time. My good friend Sam greets me, "Namaste." Meaning, "I bow to you, or to the divine spark I see in you."

Sarah's story is about letting life in. Every bit of life. Sarah's story is about making space, sanctuary space. When we make space, we are able to bring who we are—whether that be grieving or sadness or bewilderment or gladness or joy.

I was honored to participate in a Congressional Civil Rights Pilgrimage, to Selma and Montgomery and Birmingham, Alabama, to remember Bloody Sunday and the crossing of the bridge in Selma. We sat in the First Baptist Church of Montgomery.

Police Chief Kevin Murphy was not initially invited to the event. He was asked to speak only after Montgomery's mayor and director of public safety were unable to attend. And Chief Murphy went off script. He was supposed to say, simply, "Welcome to Montgomery." Instead, he said he wanted the Montgomery Police Department to be "heard in a different light than what history has recorded in years past. There's still a lot of work to do; we know that. We, the police department, need to make the first move to build that trust back in our community that was once lost because we enforced unjust laws. Those unjust laws were immoral and wrong. But you know what? It's a new day. And there's a new police department and a new Montgomery here now and on the horizon."

Chief Murphy asked Representative John Lewis, the leader of our pilgrimage, to stand and come forward. Lewis, a civil rights leader since the 1960s, was beaten on that bridge in Selma during Bloody Sunday in 1965.

Chief Murphy said simply, "We owe you an apology. When you got off the bus in Montgomery in 1961, you didn't have a friend in the police department." (At the time, the police department stood to the side as protestors were beaten and killed.) "I want you to know that you have friends in the Montgomery Police Department, that we're for you, we're with you, we want to respect the law and adhere to the law, which is what you were trying to do all along." Chief Murphy removed his badge, handing it to John Lewis. "This symbol of authority, which used to be a symbol of oppression, needs to be a symbol of reconciliation."

"It means a great deal," Lewis said later. During the 1960s Lewis had been arrested during civil rights protests across the South, but this, he said, was the first time a police chief had ever apologized to him. "I teared up. I tried to keep from crying."

We have the power to create. We can create bridges for reconciliation and second chances and peacemaking. We can create roads for mercy and generosity and justice. We can create floors for dancing and music and celebration. We create bandages for wounds and fractured spirits and broken hearts. And when we do, we create sanctuaries for safety and prayer and hope.

I do know this: When creativity spills, I live with my heart unclenched and expanded. And I am no longer a walking resentment in search of a cause.

In that Montgomery church I realized that it doesn't matter what we expect from life, but what life expects from us. As a result, we can choose to unleash the heart, in order to be our better selves.

And no one can take that away. They can demean us, belittle us, criticize us, and silence us. But no one can take that away.

"It made me feel like a human being again."

I'm reading a magazine article this afternoon, and I see a photo of the man giving the testimonial. He is referring, I think, to a church? A mandatory therapy group? A motivational seminar? A *New York Times* best seller? No.

He is a former inmate at a San Francisco prison who now works with the San Francisco Garden Project. "It made me feel like a human being again," he said of his work in a garden. The project was started by Catherine Sneed. In an eight-acre garden, prisoners grow vegetables, and that organic produce is delivered to the project, which supplies food to seniors, homeless people, and people living with AIDS. Above all, the garden is a metaphor for the healthy lives that the gardeners are trying to create for themselves.

We go to great lengths (not to mention pay good money) to find solutions to our emotional conundrums, and all this man did was put his hands in the soil, plant a seed, and watch it grow.

Did you know there are studies indicating that hospice patients actually live longer when their rooms have windows? And longer still (six to nine months) when they have access to a garden?

When I worked for the Hallmark Channel, on a program called *New Morning*, I had the privilege of shooting a segment at the Enid A. Haupt Glass Garden. Located at the New York University Medical Center, it was opened in 1958 by the Rusk Institute—where they believe that gardens are essential to healing and rehabilitation. I interviewed patients and saw firsthand what I knew to be true in my own life. The garden—an environment of plants, water, trees, sky, birds, and beauty—forces patience and slows us down. The garden is, in itself, an instrument of grace.

Your Sanctuary

Do you have a favorite public space? What about it makes you glad to be there and glad to be alive? Is it a sacred space? If so, what makes it sacred?

What role does this place play in the world near you—to combat hurry, stress, anxiety, and disquiet?

Looking back at the ingredients in chapter 5, how do you see these elements playing out in public sanctuary spaces?

Because public spaces meet the need of a variety of people, there is a communal aspect to public sanctuary. In what ways do they remind us that we are on this journey together? Or that we do, regardless of our differences, still belong to one another?

_____

_____

_____

_____

_____

_____

_____

_____

Sometimes in
Sanctuary,
Miracles Happen

You never know where you will find miracles. It could be in your own backyard.

Last month, Phil Volker completed 909 laps on a trail, walking the distance—a five-hundred-mile trek—of the Camino de Santiago, or Way of St. James, a well-known Christian pilgrimage in northern Spain. But Phil Volker wasn't in Spain—he lives on Vashon Island, Washington, where he walks most every day around a well-worn half-mile path through his ten-acre property. Phil Volker also has cancer.

If his doctors give final approval, this summer Volker will go from backyard pilgrim to actual pilgrim when he flies to Spain to walk the real deal. "I wanted to experience it," he said. "But if I don't get to go, I'm going to be happy with what I've got here. It's more than I thought I could do."

Volker's journey began three years ago when he was diagnosed with colon cancer, something he now calls the first *C* in his life. The diagnosis led him to the second *C*, the Catholic Church (more specifically St. John Vianney parish here on Vashon), where he's found meaning, support, and friendship. "Having a life-threatening obstacle, it straightens out your priorities," he says.

Volker first learned of the pilgrimage walk after he was given a copy of *The Way*, the 2012 film featuring Martin Sheen walking the Camino de Santiago. The film hooks you when you least expect it. It is a poignant and inspirational story about family, friends, and the challenges we face while navigating loss, including the loss of our expectations and dreams.

Martin Sheen plays Tom, an American doctor who comes to Saint-Jean-Pied-de-Port, France, to collect the remains of his adult son Daniel (played by Martin Sheen's real-life son Emilio Estevez), who was killed in the Pyrenees in a storm while walking the Camino de Santiago. Rather than return home, Tom decides to embark on the historical pilgrimage himself, to honor his son's desire to savor the journey. What Tom doesn't plan on is the profound impact the journey will have on him and his life in a bubble in California. In flashbacks, we learn that Daniel died estranged from his father, having embarked on a life Tom called wasteful and frivolous. In one scene Daniel tells his father, "That's just it, Dad. You don't choose a life, you live one."

That's why Volker's story resonates. He's living life. Even as life turns left.

Life seems to ignore the script we have in our mind. And when that happens, we walk. We walk toward, or we walk away. Either way, we begin a journey—a pilgrimage to find or restore or forgive or heal, or to forget or bury—or perhaps just to have the deck of our world shuffled.

Phil Volker is walking, and the Camino has become his third *C*. "It's become an international phenomenon," Volker says. "You're walking in the footsteps of millions of people who have come before you."

Believing he was too ill to travel and walk such a long distance, Volker (who is also a hiker) set about re-creating the walk closer to home. Last December his trail was blessed by

Father Marc Powell of St. John Vianney, and Volker began to walk.

Walking the trail, Volker frequently passes posts with scallop shells—the symbol of the Camino. He walks past hanging bird feeders, well-worn hunting targets in the woods, and a small stream with a line of rocks to cross it. When a dog in a neighboring yard approaches the fence, he promptly produces a treat from his pocket.

"It seems to be different every time," he says of the walk. There's a reason. Volker is seldom alone as he walks on any of his 909 laps. More than one hundred friends, family members, acquaintances, and even doctors have accompanied Volker on various legs of the walk.

Volker keeps careful records in a logbook, daily recording how far he walks (as many as six miles a day), whom he walks with, and where he would be on the actual Camino.

The walking is not only good for the soul, it seems, but also good for his health. Because recent scans have come back clean, Volker says, it bodes well for his trip to Spain. If two more scans come back clean, doctors will give him the OK to skip one chemo treatment and spend four weeks in July and August walking the Camino. He plans to walk the final one hundred kilometers to the Cathedral of Santiago de Compostela, a stretch required to receive an official certificate of completion.

Yes, Phil Volker is looking forward to what the Camino will hold, but he also says that he's already been changed on his own backyard journey: "It's really enriched my life. My life has never been richer than it is right now."

Coming to the end of a walk, Volker bends down to pick up a stone and tosses it onto a large pile of rocks in front of his home. He explains that each rock represents a prayer said either by him or a guest after finishing a walk, similar to a tradition on the real Camino.

"All of these things got prayed for," he says. "Maybe there are miracles in there that happened."

In July, Phil made it to Spain. He walked the Camino, accompanied by friends, and he received the certificate of completion. He still lives on Vashon and takes a daily walk on the trail behind his house.

About the Author

Terry Hershey is an inspirational speaker, humorist, author, dad, Protestant minister, landscape designer, and avid golfer. He lives on Vashon Island, near Seattle, Washington. His work has been featured on the Hallmark Channel, PBS, and NPR, and he is the author of *The Power of Pause* (Loyola Press) and *Soul Gardening* (Augsburg).

For additional resources—websites, practices, books, and organizations—to help you create sanctuary, or to have Terry Hershey make a presentation for your organization, contact him at www.terryhershey.com, 800-524-5370

CONTINUE THE CONVERSATION

If you enjoyed this book, then connect with Loyola Press to continue the conversation, engage with other readers, and find out about new and upcoming books from your favorite spiritual writers.

Visit us at **www.loyolapress.com** to create an account and register for our newsletters. Or scan the code to the right with your smartphone.

Connect with us through:

 Facebook
facebook.com
/loyolapress

 Twitter
twitter.com
/loyolapress

 YouTube
youtube.com
/loyolapress

ALSO BY TERRY HERSHEY

The Power of Pause
Becoming More by Doing Less

PB | $12.95 | 3546-7

In *The Power of Pause*, Hershey encourages all of us to slow down and reconnect with what's important in life.

Through 52 short chapters featuring powerful stories and meditations, inspiring quotations, and everyday opportunities for simplicity, we learn how to take back the life that God always intended for us to have—a life that revolves not so much around doing, but simply being.

ALSO AVAILABLE

Blessed By Less

PB | $13.95 | 3902-1

Blessed by Less guides readers through the process of uncluttering from a holistic perspective—spiritual, physical, and emotional—so that we can better know what to keep and what to let go.

Love Will Steer Me True

PB | $13.95 | 4143-7

Love Will Steer Me True shows how a mother and daughter swerve and weave their way into a new understanding of themselves, of their familial relationship, and of their faith.

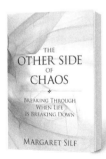

The Other Side of Chaos

PB | $13.95 | 3308-1

In *The Other Side of Chaos*, best-selling author Margaret Silf helps us look closely at the "messes" in our lives through the lens of Christian spirituality, enabling us to see the chaos of life not as something to fear or eschew, but as something to be embraced.

To order, visit us online at **www.loyolapress.com**, call 800.621.1008, or visit your local bookseller.